GALATIANS
FROM START2FINISH

MICHAEL WHITWORTH

ISBN 978-1-941972-25-0

Published by Start2Finish
Bend, Oregon 97702
start2finish.org

Printed in the United States of America

Cover Design: Evangela Creative

CONTENTS

1

NO OTHER GOSPEL

GALATIANS 1:1-10

Objective: To defend the one true gospel
and call Christians back to grace.

INTRODUCTION

In 1862, during the height of the American Civil War, the United States faced a crisis few recognized at first. Counterfeiters—taking advantage of national turmoil—were flooding the country with fake currency. Before the creation of the Secret Service, there were hundreds of types of banknotes in circulation, each designed by individual banks. This made counterfeiting extraordinarily easy. By some estimates, one-third of the money in circulation was counterfeit.

The problem wasn't that the fake bills looked obviously wrong. Many were convincing—close in design, nearly identical in feel, and passable in ordinary transactions. But small distortions in engraving, lettering, or layout made them worthless. Banks failed. Merchants lost income. Soldiers received pay they couldn't spend. What looked genuine caused financial chaos because it wasn't the real thing.

When the Secret Service was eventually formed, its agents didn't train by studying every fake bill in circulation. Instead, they spent hours examining real currency—its texture, its marks, its symmetry, its intricate details—so that any distortion, no matter how subtle, would stand out immediately. The safest way to recognize a counterfeit was to know the original by heart.

Paul writes Galatians 1:1–10 with a similar burden. The Christians in Galatia weren't rejecting the gospel outright. They were accepting a version that looked familiar but carried distortions—small enough to seem harmless, significant enough to change everything. Teachers had added requirements to the message of Christ, creating a gospel that no longer centered on grace.

Paul responds urgently because a distorted gospel, like counterfeit currency, may look close to the original, but it cannot save. His passion in these opening verses is to call the Galatians back to the pure message of Christ—the only gospel with real power, real promise, and real freedom.

EXAMINATION

Paul's opening words to the Galatians feel different from every other letter he wrote. Typically, Paul eases into his message with gratitude, encouragement, or a prayer of blessing. Even when he needs to correct a church, he usually begins by reminding them of God's work among them. But in Galatians, there is no such warm-up. Paul steps straight into the heart of the issue—even his greeting feels tight, compressed, and urgent. You can sense from the very first sentences that something is deeply wrong among these Christians and that Paul is writing with a pastor's burden and an apostle's authority.

The churches in Galatia had come to Christ through Paul's preaching. He had seen their joy firsthand, watched them turn away from idols, and witnessed the Spirit at work among them. But now, hardly after Paul has left, they are drifting in a direction that jeopardizes the gospel itself. They haven't abandoned Jesus outright. They haven't stopped gathering or singing or praying. The crisis is far subtler. They are being influenced by teachers who insist that faith in Christ is not enough—that Gentile Christians cannot be fully included in God's people unless they adopt the boundary markers of the Mosaic law. Circumcision, festival observances, and dietary practices had become requirements for "full membership." These teachers were not anti-Jesus; they were Jesus *plus*. But in Paul's mind, a Jesus-plus message becomes a Jesus-minus gospel. Additions do not enrich the good news; they dilute it until it becomes something else entirely.

Before Paul addresses the crisis, he reminds the Galatians of who he is—and more importantly, who sent him. He writes as "an apostle—not from men nor through man, but through Jesus Christ and God the Father who raised him from the dead." That is a deliberate framing. Paul's ministry did not originate from any human institution. He was not appointed by a committee in Jerusalem or endorsed by an apostolic board. His authority traces back to the risen Christ himself, who appeared to Paul, called him, and entrusted him with the message he now defends. In a letter where rival teachers are claiming superior insight, Paul begins by establishing that his calling comes directly from the One who conquered death. You may disagree with Paul, but you cannot dismiss him as merely expressing a personal opinion. He speaks on behalf of the Lord who sent him.

Paul then extends a blessing that looks simple on the surface—"Grace to you and peace"—but carries rich meaning for everything he is about to say. Grace is the very heart of the gospel: God's unearned, undeserved favor. Peace is the result of grace: reconciliation, wholeness, and restored relationship. These gifts come "from God our Father and the Lord Jesus Christ," not from law-keeping or ethnic markers. Paul subtly reminds them that the Christian life begins and continues through God's generosity, not human achievement. The agitators in Galatia are offering a path toward acceptance through performance. Paul counters right away: everything that matters comes from God's grace.

Paul briefly summarizes the gospel in verse 4, and the summary is so rich that it could serve as the thesis of the entire letter. Christ "gave himself for our sins to deliver us from the present evil age." That is the gospel in miniature. Christ did not merely teach or inspire. He gave himself—his very life—in a self-sacrificing act meant to rescue helpless people. And what he rescues us from is not merely guilt or shame but the entire world order dominated by sin and death. Through Christ's work, Christians are transferred out of the realm of the "present evil age" and into the new creation of God's kingdom. Every phrase in this summary pushes us back to grace. Salvation is God's work on behalf of sinful people, not the product of human effort. It is deliverance, not self-improvement; rescue, not reward.

Up to this point, Paul has been firm but not confrontational. But everything changes in verse 6. Without warning, Paul expresses his astonishment: "I am astonished that you are so quickly deserting him who called you in the grace of Christ." We feel the depth of Paul's emotion here—not anger as much as disbelief and grief. These Christians had experienced the grace of Christ, and yet they were turning aside from the God who had called them. Notice Paul's wording: they are not merely deserting a doctrine; they are deserting *Him*. To distort the gospel is to step away from God himself. That is Paul's pastoral burden. He is watching people he loves slowly detach themselves from the God who saved them, and he cannot remain silent.

Paul describes their drift as turning to "a different gospel," and then immediately clarifies that such a gospel "is really no gospel at all." There is only one message that brings salvation. Anything that adds to the finished work of Christ subtracts from it. The teachers influencing Galatia were not encouraging sin; they were encouraging law-keeping. They were not rejecting Christ; they were simply adding the law to him. But Paul will not allow the gospel to be mixed with anything that undermines grace. In his eyes, the issue is not small. It is not minor disagreement. It is the difference between a message that saves and a message that enslaves.

That is why Paul's language intensifies in verses 8–9. He says that even if he, or an angel from heaven, were to preach a gospel contrary to the one he originally proclaimed, that messenger should be "accursed." This is one of the strongest statements Paul ever makes. But he makes it because the gospel is not his possession to edit or adapt. It is God's revelation, and its purity must be protected at all costs. A corrupted gospel leads to spiritual ruin because it directs people away from the sufficiency of Christ. Paul repeats the warning a second time to show that he is not reacting impulsively. He is deadly serious: eternal consequences are at stake.

The final verse of the paragraph reveals another dimension of Paul's concern. The agitators likely accused Paul of preaching an "easy" gospel to gain approval from Gentiles. Perhaps they suggested that Paul removed circumcision requirements to make Christianity more attractive. Paul responds with a rhetorical question: "Am I now seeking the approval of man, or of God?" If Paul were trying to please people, he would preach a different message—one that would win applause rather than opposition. Instead, the gospel he proclaims consistently gets him into trouble. It leads to conflict, not comfort. It provokes resistance, not popularity. Paul insists that a servant of Christ cannot shape his message according to human approval. The gospel is not a product to be marketed; it is a revelation to be faithfully guarded.

When we step back and look at the whole paragraph, Paul's concern becomes clear. The Galatians are drifting from grace, not out of defiance but out of confusion. They are allowing others to persuade them that Christ is insufficient. Paul appeals to them with a mixture of authority, urgency, and affection because he knows what is at stake. If they abandon the gospel of grace, they abandon the God who gave it. If they trade the freedom of Christ for the requirements of the law, they trade life for bondage. If they place confidence in their own works, they lose confidence in Christ.

Galatians 1:1–10, then, is not a burst of anger—it is a plea. It is a minister calling his people back to the truth. It is an apostle defending the glory of Christ's work. It is a friend reminding them of the grace they once received with joy. And it is God, through Paul, declaring that the gospel is precious and must not be altered. The message that saves must be preserved, protected, and cherished, because in the gospel Christians meet the God who calls them, loves them, and delivers them through Christ's self-giving work.

APPLICATION

1. The true gospel anchors Christians in grace, not performance

Paul's astonishment in Galatians 1 reminds us that it is possible to drift from grace without realizing it. The Christians in Galatia did not set out to abandon God; they simply allowed subtle expectations to creep into their understanding of salvation. Something similar can happen today. Christians may begin to measure their standing before God by spiritual habits, church involvement, or moral effort. All of these are important, but none of them establish or secure our relationship with God. Paul teaches that the Christian life begins and continues with grace—a gift received, not a status earned. When Christians remember that Christ gave himself "to deliver us," they can rest in the assurance of God's love without trying to prove themselves worthy. Grace does not minimize obedience; it sets obedience in its rightful place as the grateful response to God's unearned kindness.

2. The gospel must remain pure because additions ultimately distort it

The crisis in Galatia was not caused by people who rejected Jesus but by people who added to him. They insisted that Gentile Christians adopt certain practices before they could belong fully to God's family. Paul recognized this as a threat because the moment the gospel is supplemented, it is reshaped into something else. Modern versions of this temptation often take the form of cultural expectations, unspoken rules, or ideas that elevate human effort above God's work in Christ. The church must guard the gospel with the same seriousness Paul expresses. This does not mean avoiding careful thinking or resisting every form of teaching; it means refusing to let anything compete with Christ's finished work. When Christians hold tightly to the gospel of grace, they protect the church from drifting into forms of faith defined more by human achievement than divine mercy.

3. Following Christ sometimes requires resisting pressure to please people

Paul's insistence that he is "not seeking the approval of man" speaks to a struggle many Christians face. Cultural pressure, family expectations, or personal desires can make it tempting to soften or adjust the message of Christ. The gospel calls for humility, repentance, and trust in God's grace, but those truths are not always popular. Paul shows that faithfulness to Christ demands courage. Christians are not called to be harsh or combative, but they are called to be steadfast. The desire to please people can lead to compromises that chip away at the heart of the gospel. Paul models a better way: speak truth with love, maintain conviction with humility, and remember that the ultimate goal is not human approval but faithfulness to the God who calls.

4. The gospel creates confidence because it rests on Christ's finished work

The question behind many distorted gospels is simple and painful: "Am I doing enough to be right with God?" That fear can push Christians to look inward instead of upward, anchoring their hope in effort rather than grace. Paul teaches that confidence in the Christian life comes from trusting what Christ has already accomplished. The gospel does not call people to build their own righteousness; it calls them to receive Christ's righteousness. This truth frees Christians from the anxiety of constant self-evaluation and invites them into the peace that comes from resting in God's promise.

Obedience flows from that confidence, not as a means of earning favor but as a response to love already given.

CONCLUSION

Paul's opening words to the Galatians confront Christians with a choice that remains urgent today: either we cling to the gospel of grace, or we drift toward a message that places confidence in our own effort. There is no middle ground. Paul does not rebuke the Galatians because they have rejected Jesus, but because they have allowed additions to creep in—additions that threaten to undo their freedom. His urgent tone is the voice of a shepherd protecting his church and an apostle guarding the truth entrusted to him.

The gospel Paul preached is the gospel Christians still need: Christ gave himself to rescue us, and that gift is complete. Nothing needs to be added. Nothing can be improved. To desert that message is to desert the God who calls, but to hold fast to it is to stand firmly in the grace and peace God delights to give. Galatians begins with a warning, but it is a warning meant to lead us back to the joy of the one true gospel.

REFLECTION

1. How does Paul's urgency in this passage challenge the way you think about the importance of preserving the gospel's purity?

2. Where are you most tempted to measure your relationship with God by your performance rather than his grace?

3. How does Paul's summary of the gospel in verse 4 shape your understanding of what Christ accomplished for you?

4. What subtle "additions" to the gospel do you think Christians today are most vulnerable to believing?

5. In what ways does the desire for human approval pull your heart away from the simplicity of Christ's grace?

6. What does it look like for you to rest confidently in what Christ has already done rather than in what you can do?

DISCUSSION

1. Why does Paul begin this letter without a thanksgiving section, and what does that reveal about the seriousness of the issue?

2. How does Paul's claim that his apostleship is "not from men nor through man" shape the authority of his message?

3. Why is a "different gospel" really no gospel at all, even when it still includes the name of Jesus?

4. What does Paul mean when he says the Galatians are "deserting him who called you"? How is the issue relational, not just doctrinal?

5. Why does Paul pronounce a curse even on himself or an angel if they preach a different gospel?

6. What does it look like today to refuse the pressure to please people and instead remain faithful to the gospel of grace?

2

A GOSPEL REVEALED, A LIFE TRANSFORMED

GALATIANS 1:11-24

Objective: To show that the gospel is revealed by God, transforms lives, and confirms Paul's authentic calling.

INTRODUCTION

In 1918, during the final months of World War I, a young British soldier named Wilfred Owen was stationed on the Western Front. Today he is remembered as one of the greatest war poets of the twentieth century, but his transformation into a poet was not the result of formal training or literary circles. Something far more disruptive shaped him.

Earlier in the war, Owen suffered a traumatic shell explosion that left him concussed, disoriented, and emotionally shattered. He was sent to a hospital in Edinburgh, where he encountered another poet, Siegfried Sassoon, whose own experiences had ignited a fierce protest against the war. Their conversations awakened something in Owen. He began writing with startling honesty about the suffering of soldiers, the horrors of trench warfare, and the cost of misguided nationalism.

When he returned to the front, Owen was not the same man who had enlisted. His voice, perspective, and purpose had changed. The war he once entered with patriotic enthusiasm now stirred in him a burden to speak truth, expose illusion, and give voice to the voiceless. His transformation was unmistakable, and the poems he wrote in those final months have shaped generations.

Paul tells his story in Galatians 1:11–24 with a similar clarity of transformation—though the change in Paul was even more dramatic and divinely shaped. He had once been consumed by zeal, driven by tradition, and convinced he was defending God's honor by opposing Christians. But a revelation of Jesus overturned his convictions, redirected his passion, and reshaped the entire trajectory of his life. His message did not originate from human influence or institutional authority; it came from the risen Christ who called him by grace.

In this passage, Paul shows the Galatians that the gospel is not a human idea, and his ministry is not the product of human training. The gospel is God's revelation, powerful enough to transform the most unlikely person—and gracious enough to do so.

EXAMINATION

Paul continues his letter to the Galatians by turning from the danger they face to the story that shaped his own life. If the opening ten verses were a warning, these next verses are a testimony. Paul is not simply arguing for the gospel's truth—he is showing how the gospel invaded his world and remade him from the inside out. Galatians 1:11–24 is Paul's personal history, not to draw attention to himself, but to demonstrate that the message he preaches comes directly from God and carries the power to transform even the most unlikely of people.

Paul begins by repeating a claim he had hinted at in the letter's opening: the gospel he preached "is not man's gospel." He does not mean that the gospel is opposed to humanity, but that its origin is divine rather than human. No group of teachers trained Paul in this message. He did not inherit it from Jewish tradition. He did not learn it around a campfire from the apostles in Jerusalem. Instead, Paul insists that he "did not receive it from any man, nor was [he] taught it," but that he "received it through a revelation of Jesus Christ." This bold claim sets his gospel apart from the message of the agitators, who seem confident that their version of Christianity carries ancient approval based on Mosaic law and centuries of tradition.

Paul is careful to explain that his argument is not a matter of pride or ego. He is not asserting that he possesses deeper spiritual insight than others.

What matters is that the gospel comes from God himself—not human speculation, cultural custom, or religious expectation. If the gospel were merely a human idea, then adjustments and additions might be acceptable. Human ideas can evolve; divine truth cannot. Paul tells his story, because in his story the Galatians can see what God has done and hear how God speaks.

Paul then looks backward, inviting the Galatians to remember the person he used to be. He reminds them that he once "persecuted the church of God violently and tried to destroy it." This is not exaggeration. Acts tells us that Paul traveled from city to city hunting Christians, dragging them from their homes, and approving of their imprisonment. Before his conversion, Paul viewed Christians as a dangerous threat to the purity of Israel's faith, and he was determined to stop the movement in its tracks. He had built a reputation as a zealous defender of the Pharisaic traditions, devoted to the law, and committed to stamping out anything that resembled a threat to Israel's covenant identity.

This part of Paul's story matters because it demonstrates how unlikely his transformation was. A person who is deeply committed to destroying something rarely becomes its champion. When someone changes course that dramatically, we naturally wonder what caused it. Paul acknowledges that there was nothing in his upbringing, his education, or his early life that pointed him toward Christ. In fact, everything in his background pulled him in the opposite direction. His story shows that the gospel did not come from his upbringing or from gradual spiritual growth. It came from a revelation that broke into his life and turned it upside down.

Paul describes that moment with remarkable simplicity: "But when he who had set me apart before I was born, and who called me by his grace, was pleased to reveal his Son to me…" With those words, Paul reframes his entire past. The God he once resisted had been at work in his life all along. Paul had not been wandering aimlessly; he had been moving toward a moment God ordained. He had been "set apart" before birth—not because he was worthy, but because God had a purpose for him. And the God who set him apart also "called" him, not with condemnation, but with grace.

Paul's language here echoes the prophets. Jeremiah was set apart in the womb, Isaiah called from before birth. Paul sees his calling as part of a long story of God choosing and shaping unlikely servants. But the heart of Paul's turning point is this: God "was pleased to reveal his Son." Revelation is not merely information; it is unveiling. Paul had known about Jesus before his encounter on the Damascus road—he just believed Jesus was a fraud. The revelation changed everything. Suddenly, Paul realized that the crucified one was the risen Lord, the fulfillment of God's promises, and the cornerstone of the new covenant. The gospel did not come to Paul through argument or persuasion; it came through an encounter with Christ that redefined reality.

After this encounter, Paul did not rush to Jerusalem for approval or instruction. Instead, he went into Arabia and then returned to Damascus. The details are sparse, but Paul's point is clear: he did not build his message on the foundation of another apostle's teaching. His understanding of the gospel developed in the presence of God, shaped by prayer, reflection, and the Spirit's guidance. This does not imply that Paul lived in isolation or disregarded the fellowship of other Christians. Rather, it means the gospel he preached was not secondhand. It came from the same Christ whom Peter, James, and John followed.

Paul eventually visited Jerusalem, but not immediately. After three years, he went to meet Cephas (Peter) and stayed with him for fifteen days. The timeframe is important. Fifteen days is long enough for fellowship and conversation but far too short for extensive theological training. Paul also met James, the Lord's brother. These are not casual details; they serve Paul's larger point. The leaders in Jerusalem recognized Paul's ministry but did not shape or authorize his message. The gospel was consistent because its source was the same: Christ.

Paul is careful to emphasize his honesty here, saying, "In what I am writing to you, before God, I do not lie!" His oath underscores the sincerity of his account and the trustworthiness of his testimony. The Galatians needed to know that Paul was not exaggerating or crafting a narrative for his own benefit. He is telling the truth about his past to protect them from the kind of teaching that would lead them back into bondage.

After leaving Jerusalem, Paul traveled into the regions of Syria and Cilicia. He preached in places far removed from the centers of Jewish influence. The churches in Judea heard reports about him, but many had not met him personally. Instead, they heard the remarkable news: "He who used to persecute us is now preaching the faith he once tried to destroy." Paul's transformation became a testimony to the power of the gospel. The message that once enraged him now compelled him. The people he once hunted became his family. The faith he once despised became his life's mission.

The story ends with a beautiful conclusion: "They glorified God because of me." This is the heartbeat of Paul's entire testimony. He is not telling his story to glorify himself, defend his reputation, or gather sympathy. He is telling it because the gospel's origin, power, and truth are at stake. His transformation was so profound that it forced people to look beyond him and see the hand of God. Paul wanted the Galatians to know that the gospel he preached had reshaped him from the ground up, and it could do the same for them—if they remained faithful to it.

Across these fourteen verses, Paul weaves together three threads: the divine origin of the gospel, the transforming power of grace, and the authenticity of his calling. The gospel did not begin with human wisdom. It intruded into Paul's life with a force that only God could provide. And that same gospel took a violent persecutor and turned him into a passionate preacher. The Galatians needed to see that their own story was part of that same grace. They had been called by the same God, saved by the same Christ, and filled with the same Spirit. To abandon the gospel now would not only distort the message; it would ignore the very power that had reshaped Paul's life.

Paul's story stands as a reminder that the gospel is more than doctrine—it is transformation. It takes those who oppose Christ and makes them servants of Christ. It takes those who trust in human tradition and teaches them to trust in grace. And it takes those who drift away and calls them back to the truth. By the end of the passage, the issue is clear: the gospel Paul defends is the gospel God revealed. It is the message that changed him, and it is the message that will sustain the Galatians—if they will hold fast to the grace that first called them.

APPLICATION

1. God's gospel cannot be reshaped because it comes from him, not us

Paul anchors his entire story in the truth that the gospel is not a human invention. He did not brainstorm it, refine it, or inherit it through tradition. It broke into his life through revelation. This matters because Christians today face constant pressure to adapt or soften the gospel to fit the expectations of culture, family, or personal preference. But a message that originates with God cannot be revised by people. When Christians remember that the gospel begins with God's initiative, they gain confidence to hold firmly to it even when it is countercultural or unpopular. The authority of the gospel does not rest on the skill of those who preach it or the approval of those who hear it. It rests on the God who revealed it and the Christ who gave himself to accomplish it.

2. God's grace transforms even the most unlikely stories

Paul's transformation from persecutor to preacher is one of the most dramatic turnarounds in Scripture. He reminds the Galatians of his violent past not to magnify his shame but to magnify God's grace. The message is simple and profound: no one is beyond the reach of the gospel. Christ met Paul in his rage, overturned his assumptions, and rewrote his future. Christians today can take comfort in this truth. Whether dealing with personal guilt, praying for a wandering friend, or feeling discouraged by long-standing struggles, Paul's story shows that God delights in transforming unlikely hearts. Grace does not simply modify behavior; it reshapes identity. And the same God who pursued Paul continues to meet people in the middle of their resistance, revealing Christ and creating new life.

3. Faithfulness sometimes means standing firm without waiting for human approval

Paul emphasizes that he did not consult with the Jerusalem apostles before beginning his ministry. His point is not that Christians should reject wisdom or fellowship, but that faithfulness to Christ cannot hinge on human validation. In a world where acceptance often feels essential, Paul's example encourages Christians to follow Christ even when affirmation is slow, uncertain, or absent. Many forms of obedience—repenting of sin, speaking truth gently but clearly, resisting harmful habits, or maintaining integrity—may be misunderstood by others. Paul reminds us that our calling comes from God, and our confidence must rest there. Faithfulness grows when Christians are willing to obey even when applause is not guaranteed and recognition is delayed.

4. A transformed life points others to God, not ourselves

Paul ends this section by saying that the churches in Judea "glorified God because of me." His story became a window through which others could see the power of grace at work. This offers a gentle but important reminder: the purpose of a Christian's testimony is not to showcase personal success but to direct attention toward the God who saves. When Christians share how Christ has changed them—how he has healed what was broken, forgiven what was sinful, or guided what was uncertain—the goal is not self-promotion. It is worship. Paul's example invites Christians to live in such a way that others want to praise God, not us. A transformed life becomes a quiet but compelling witness to the One who reveals his Son and calls us by grace.

CONCLUSION

Galatians 1:11–24 gives a glimpse into the power of the gospel through the story of a man whose life was unexpectedly and completely transformed. Paul offers his testimony not to center attention on himself, but to reassure the Galatians that the message he preached did not originate in human wisdom or tradition. It came from God, revealed through Christ, and confirmed by a transformation so dramatic that even distant churches glorified God because of it.

Paul's journey from persecutor to preacher reminds Christians that the gospel is not merely information—it is transformation. It reaches into hardened hearts, reorders priorities, and creates a new identity grounded in grace. And because this gospel is rooted in God's initiative rather than human invention, Christians can trust its truth, depend on its power, and build their lives on its promises. Paul's story stands as an enduring witness that the God who revealed his Son to him continues to call, redeem, and reshape Christians today.

REFLECTION

1. How does Paul's description of receiving the gospel "through a revelation of Jesus Christ" deepen your understanding of its authority?

2. Where do you see evidence of God's grace transforming unexpected places in your own story?

3. What obstacles make it difficult for you to rest in God's calling rather than seeking human approval?

4. In what ways does Paul's past remind you that no one is outside the reach of God's mercy?

5. How does Paul's independence from the Jerusalem apostles shape your view of the gospel's consistency and reliability?

6. What would it look like for your life to lead others to glorify God because of what he has done in you?

DISCUSSION

1. Why does Paul emphasize so strongly that he did not receive the gospel from any person?

2. How does Paul's past as a persecutor strengthen his argument that the gospel is divine in origin?

3. What does Paul's extended time away from Jerusalem teach us about the development of his ministry?

4. Why is it significant that the churches in Judea glorified God rather than Paul when they heard his story?

5. How does Paul's calling echo the call of Old Testament prophets like Jeremiah and Isaiah?

6. How does this passage challenge Christians today to hold firmly to the gospel even when cultural pressure pushes toward compromise?

3

ONE GOSPEL, ONE MISSION

GALATIANS 2:1-10

Objective: To see how the apostles affirmed one gospel, upheld Christian freedom, and partnered in God's mission.

INTRODUCTION

In 1846, the United States Congress established the Smithsonian Institution, a national museum and research center intended to advance knowledge and preserve history. When the first crates of scientific specimens and cultural artifacts began arriving from around the world, curators faced a major problem: different expeditions had used different cataloging systems. Labels didn't match. Descriptions conflicted. Measurements varied. In some cases, two explorers described the same object in completely different ways.

The confusion made it difficult to build a unified collection. If one scientist called a specimen by one name and another used a different classification, how could the Smithsonian preserve accuracy? Over time the institution created one harmonized standard—agreed-upon terminology, shared measurements, and a single system for describing artifacts. That standard allowed researchers from different backgrounds to work together without confusion. Their unity didn't come from their identical methods or personal histories; it came from a shared commitment to the same source of truth.

Paul's account in Galatians 2:1–10 tells a similar story—though with far higher stakes. Early Christianity spread rapidly across cultures, languages, and regions. It would have been easy for different leaders to preach competing messages or shape the gospel according to their own backgrounds. But when Paul traveled to Jerusalem fourteen years after his conversion, the apostles recognized immediately that the message he preached was the same gospel revealed to them. Their unity didn't come from shared personalities or identical ministries. It came from a shared commitment to the truth God had revealed in Christ.

This passage shows that the gospel did not fracture into regional versions or cultural adaptations. It remained one message, one mission, and one movement, upheld by leaders who saw the grace of God at work in one another. And because they guarded that unity, Christians today can be confident that the gospel they believe is the same gospel that shaped the first century church.

EXAMINATION

As Paul continues his autobiographical defense in Galatians, he moves from the story of his conversion to the story of his calling. The Galatians needed to know not simply that Paul was transformed, but that the message he preached was in complete harmony with the gospel proclaimed in Jerusalem. The agitators influencing them likely claimed that Paul's gospel was incomplete or independent, perhaps even disconnected from the teaching of the "real" apostles. Galatians 2:1–10 dismantles that accusation. Here Paul tells the story of his second visit to Jerusalem and shows that the gospel he preaches is the gospel the apostles publicly affirmed.

This passage is one of the most important in the New Testament for understanding early Christian unity. It shows that the leaders of the Jerusalem church and Paul did not preach competing messages. The gospel was not fragmented. There was no "Jerusalem version" for Jewish Christians and a "Paul version" for Gentile Christians. God revealed one gospel, entrusted that gospel to the apostles, and empowered that gospel to form one united people. Galatians 2:1–10 is Paul's way of inviting the Galatians into the story so that they can see the roots of that unity and understand how essential it is to Christian identity.

Paul begins by noting that it had been fourteen years since his conversion when God prompted him to travel back to Jerusalem. The wording is purposeful: Paul went "because of a revelation." This trip was not politically motivated or pressured by other leaders. It was not the result of insecurity, nor was it an attempt to gain the approval of those who ministered before him. God directed him to go. Even his travel companions are significant: Barnabas, a respected Jewish Christian, and Titus, a Greek Christian who had never been circumcised. Their presence embodied the very question under debate: must Gentile Christians adopt Jewish ceremonial identity markers to belong fully to the people of God?

When Paul arrived in Jerusalem, he presented the gospel he preached among the Gentiles to "those who seemed influential." This phrase might sound dismissive at first, but Paul's point is not to diminish their importance. He wants the Galatians to understand that he did not view the other apostles as rivals. Their influence was real, but it did not intimidate him. Nor did it change the source of his message. Paul presented his gospel privately so that their conversation could focus on truth, not on rumor or public pressure. He wanted to "make sure [he] was not running or had not run in vain." That phrase does not mean Paul doubted his gospel. Rather, he cared about the unity of the church. If competing messages circulated among Christians, the mission would fracture, and the movement would stumble. Paul sought unity, not approval.

The most striking piece of evidence for the gospel's unity comes in verse 3: "But even Titus… was not forced to be circumcised." Titus is the living, breathing proof that Gentiles do not need to take on the identity markers of the Mosaic law in order to belong fully to God's family. If the apostles in Jerusalem had believed otherwise, Titus would have been the first to know. Instead, they affirmed that Titus, uncircumcised as he was, stood fully within the people of God because of Christ. That moment is not merely an anecdote—it is a declaration of Christian freedom.

Paul then describes the pressure that had come from "false brothers secretly brought in." These individuals were not genuine Christians, although they portrayed themselves as such. They attempted to spy out the freedom Christians have in Christ in order to drag them back into bondage. Their teaching threatened the heart of the gospel. If Gentile Christians had to become Jews in order to belong, then the sufficiency of Christ would be undermined. The new creation would become a modified form of the old covenant rather than the fulfillment of God's promises in Christ.

Paul's response is firm: "To them we did not yield in submission even for a moment." His language echoes battlefield resolve. He stood his ground because the gospel was at stake. He resisted not to assert personal independence, but to protect the freedom of Christians who had been redeemed by Christ. If Paul had conceded, even in one isolated case, the door would have opened for a gospel shaped more by cultural custom than by God's grace. His resistance preserved the truth of the gospel not only for Titus, but for every Christian who would follow.

The next movement in the passage turns toward mutual recognition. Paul says that "those who seemed influential added nothing to me." Again, he is not downplaying their role. He is emphasizing that the gospel he preached was complete and did not require correction from those who had walked with Jesus in his earthly ministry. The message Paul received by revelation matched perfectly with the message the apostles had proclaimed since Pentecost. This unity is stunning when we consider how different their backgrounds were. Peter, James, and John were Jewish fishermen rooted in the traditions of Israel. Paul was a Pharisee with intense zeal for the law. Yet when Christ called each of them, he formed one gospel in their hearts and one mission for their lives.

Not only did the apostles affirm Paul's message; they also recognized the grace given to him. They saw that God had entrusted Paul with a particular mission—to preach Christ among the Gentiles. In the same way, Peter had been entrusted with preaching Christ among the Jews. This division was not a matter of disagreement but of partnership. The apostles understood their roles in God's broader plan: one gospel, two apostolic missions, united under one Lord. Their handshake in verse 9, often called "the right hand of fellowship," formalized that partnership. It is not a casual greeting but a public recognition of shared mission, shared message, and shared trust.

Paul's story ends with a brief but meaningful reminder: the apostles asked him to "remember the poor." For Paul, that request was not burdensome but natural. The gospel does not simply deliver people from sin; it also forms a community marked by love, service, and compassion. This closing note ties together the themes of the passage. The gospel unites people who once stood apart. The gospel frees Christians from old divisions. The gospel reshapes human relationships with mercy and generosity. And the gospel sends Christians into the world with both conviction and compassion.

Across these ten verses, Paul makes it clear that:

- the gospel he preached was revealed by God,
- the apostles in Jerusalem affirmed its truth,
- Titus stands as living proof of Christian freedom,
- false brothers attempted to distort the gospel,
- unity was preserved through steadfastness,
- and the church's mission extended outward with love.

Galatians 2:1–10 is not merely Paul's defense of his ministry. It is an invitation for the Galatians—and for Christians today—to see how God knit the early church together through one gospel and one Spirit. There was no competition among the apostles, no divided message, no fragmentation in God's plan. The gospel they preached was Christ alone, received by grace, embraced through faith, and lived out in a community shaped by love.

And because it is the same gospel Paul defends today, Christians can hold to it with confidence. The unity of the early church around this message remains the foundation of Christian identity. What God revealed to Paul and affirmed through the apostles is the message that continues to liberate, transform, and unite Christians in every generation.

APPLICATION

1. The gospel unites Christians across background, culture, and calling

Paul's story in Galatians 2:1–10 shows that unity is not built on shared traditions, identical experiences, or personality similarities. It is built on the one gospel revealed by God. Jewish Christians in Jerusalem and Gentile Christians across the Roman world stood together because Christ brought them together. This unity did not require uniformity. Peter served mainly among Jews, and Paul served mainly among Gentiles. Yet their message was the same and their mission complementary. Christians today need this reminder. Churches come with different histories, strengths, and challenges, but unity is found in the gospel, not in sameness. When Christians keep the message of grace at the center, they discover that differences become opportunities for partnership rather than sources of division.

2. Christian freedom is worth protecting because it rests on Christ's finished work

Titus stands in this passage as a quiet but powerful reminder that Christians are not defined by external markers but by faith in Christ. Paul refused to allow anyone to pressure Titus into circumcision because such a requirement would compromise the gospel's sufficiency. That same temptation still appears in new forms—pressures to meet cultural expectations, assumptions about what "real" faith must look like, or traditions that quietly claim authority equal to Scripture. Christian freedom is not the freedom to do whatever one wants. It is the freedom to stand in what Christ has already done. When Christians guard that freedom, they protect the gospel from becoming tangled in human expectations and ensure that grace remains at the center of their identity.

3. Faithfulness sometimes means holding firm when others misunderstand or oppose us

Paul's refusal to yield "even for a moment" shows a kind of courage that does not chase conflict but refuses to surrender truth. Some of the pressure he faced came from false Christians who wanted to reshape the gospel. Some likely came from sincere Christians who were unsure how Gentiles fit into God's plan. Paul stood firm in both cases because the gospel—not popularity or comfort—was his priority. Christians today often find themselves in similar places. Holding firm may bring misunderstanding at work, confusion among friends, or questions from family. Faithfulness requires wisdom, humility, and gentleness, but it also requires courage. Paul's example encourages Christians to remain anchored in truth even when the ground around them feels shaky.

4. The gospel produces communities shaped by compassion and generosity

The apostles' final request—"remember the poor"—reveals the heart of the gospel at work. The unity Paul defended was not abstract; it took shape through love. The Jerusalem Christians, facing famine and hardship, needed help, and Paul gladly committed to gathering support. The gospel does not unite people simply in doctrine; it unites them in care. When Christians serve one another, bear one another's burdens, and meet practical needs, they show the world what grace looks like in action. A church shaped by the gospel is a church where generosity flows naturally—not because of pressure, but because Christ has first given himself for us. In a world fractured by self-interest, gospel-driven compassion becomes a powerful testimony to the God who unites and restores his people.

CONCLUSION

Galatians 2:1–10 offers a remarkable window into the unity and clarity of the gospel in the earliest days of the church. Paul's journey to Jerusalem was not an appeal for permission or authority—it was a moment when God revealed his faithfulness in bringing different leaders together around one message. Titus stood as living evidence that Gentile Christians belonged fully to God's people without adopting the Mosaic law. Paul's firm resistance protected that truth, while the apostles' endorsement confirmed it.

The early church did not grow because its leaders were identical, but because they trusted the same gospel and recognized the same grace at work in one another. Their partnership ensured that Christians from any background could stand together in Christ without barriers or divisions. This passage reminds us that unity is not built on tradition or preference but on the gospel itself. And that same gospel continues to unite, sustain, and guide Christians today.

REFLECTION

1. How does Paul's God-directed trip to Jerusalem shape your understanding of spiritual discernment and obedience?

2. Where do you see Christian unity threatened today, and how does this passage call you to pursue unity rooted in the gospel?

3. What does Titus' example teach you about the nature of Christian identity?

4. Where might you need to stand firm in the truth of the gospel, even when pressured to compromise?

5. How does the apostles' recognition of God's grace in Paul challenge you to notice God's work in others?

6. In what ways can you practice "remembering the poor" as a natural expression of the gospel?

DISCUSSION

1. Why does Paul emphasize that he went to Jerusalem "because of a revelation"?

2. How does the decision not to compel Titus to be circumcised clarify the heart of the gospel?

3. What does Paul's resistance to false teachers show about the importance of guarding Christian freedom?

4. How do the actions of Peter, James, and John demonstrate unity rather than hierarchy?

5. Why is it significant that Paul's gospel did not need to be corrected or expanded by the Jerusalem apostles?

6. How does this passage challenge modern churches to balance unity, truth, and compassion?

4

WALKING IN STEP WITH THE GOSPEL

GALATIANS 2:11-21

Objective: To show how the gospel demands integrity, grounds justification in faith, and reshapes identity in Christ.

INTRODUCTION

In 1955, during the early days of the American civil rights movement, a young pastor named Fred Shuttlesworth accepted a call to serve a church in Birmingham, Alabama—at the time one of the most segregated cities in the country. Shuttlesworth knew that racial inequality was deeply embedded not only in public life but also in many churches. Sunday assemblies were often separated by skin color, and attempts to challenge the practice were met with hostility.

On Christmas night that same year, a white supremacist group placed sixteen sticks of dynamite beside the wall of his home, right next to his bedroom. The explosion tore through the house, ripping doors from their hinges and collapsing walls. Yet Shuttlesworth walked out of the wreckage unharmed. He later said he felt that God had spared him for a purpose: "The Lord knew I lived in that house, and the Lord knew what he wanted me to do."

The bombing did not silence him. Instead, he spoke even more boldly against the hypocrisy of a system that claimed Christian faith while denying

Christian fellowship. Shuttlesworth's conviction was simple: a gospel that reconciled people to God must also reconcile people to one another. Any division that contradicted that truth had to be confronted—openly, lovingly, and courageously.

Galatians 2:11–21 records a similar moment of courageous confrontation—not over race, but over table fellowship between Jewish and Gentile Christians. When Peter withdrew from eating with Gentiles, Paul saw more than a social offense. He saw a denial of the gospel's truth. Paul confronted him not to shame him, but to defend the heart of the message they both preached: Christians are justified by faith, united in Christ, and called to live in a way that reflects that unity.

This passage shows that the gospel must shape not only what Christians believe but how they live—and sometimes faithfulness requires the courage to call inconsistencies back into line with the truth of Christ.

EXAMINATION

Galatians 2:11–21 is one of the most pivotal moments in Paul's entire letter, and arguably one of the most dramatic scenes in the New Testament. After describing his unity with the Jerusalem apostles in the previous passage, Paul now recounts an incident that shows that gospel unity is not automatic. It must be protected, lived out, and defended even among leaders who agree theologically. This is where the story of Galatians becomes intensely personal. It is the moment when Paul confronted Peter—not privately, not quietly, but publicly—because Peter's actions undermined the truth of the gospel.

This passage gives insight into the heart of the controversy in Galatia. The issue was not simply circumcision or dietary rules. It was the deeper question of who belongs to God's family and on what basis. When Peter withdrew from eating with Gentile Christians, his behavior suggested that faith in Christ was not enough—that full fellowship still depended on following the boundary markers of the Mosaic law. In Paul's eyes, this was not a minor relational misstep. It was a denial of the gospel's core truth.

Paul's retelling of this confrontation is not an attempt to embarrass Peter. It is an invitation for the Galatians to see that even an apostle can falter when cultural pressure becomes strong. But even more importantly, Paul uses the incident to teach the church that the gospel is not merely something they believe; it is something they must practice. The truth of justification by faith is not only a doctrine for debates—it shapes table fellowship, identity, relationships, and daily life.

Paul begins by recalling how Peter came to Antioch, a vibrant, mixed Jewish-Gentile congregation. Peter had no problem eating with Gentile Christians at first. He understood, as Acts 10–11 shows, that Gentiles were fully accepted by God through faith in Christ. He had defended this truth in Jerusalem. He had eaten with Cornelius and his household. He had even argued publicly that God makes no distinction between Jew and Gentile. But when certain men came "from James," Peter's courage faltered. Out of fear of criticism, he separated himself from Gentile Christians. He withdrew from the very table where grace was supposed to be experienced.

Peter's withdrawal might seem small on the surface—a change in lunch arrangements, a shift in social comfort zones. But Paul saw the deeper problem. By refusing to eat with Gentiles, Peter was signaling that they were somehow incomplete Christians unless they adopted Jewish customs. His behavior suggested that table fellowship was based on cultural identity rather than faith in Christ. And where Peter led, others followed. "The rest of the Jews acted hypocritically along with him," Paul says. Even Barnabas, Paul's longtime ministry partner and advocate for Gentile inclusion, was swept up in the pressure.

Paul uses a critical phrase to describe what went wrong: "they were not walking in step with the truth of the gospel." This is one of the most important lines in Galatians. It means that the gospel is not just a belief Christians affirm; it is a way they must live. Truth shapes behavior. Doctrine shapes decisions. The gospel is not merely about how we are saved but about how we treat one another. When Peter separated himself, he was not committing a ceremonial violation—he was denying, in practice, the equality that Christ had won for both Jew and Gentile. His actions contradicted the very gospel he believed with his heart and preached with his mouth.

Paul's confrontation was direct: "If you, though a Jew, live like a Gentile and not like a Jew, how can you force Gentiles to live like Jews?" In other words, Peter had already abandoned the old restrictions for himself. He lived in the freedom Christ provided. But by withdrawing, he created the impression that Gentiles were second-class Christians until they adopted Jewish customs. Paul insisted that this was incompatible with the gospel. If Peter lived like a Gentile, he could not require Gentiles to live like Jews.

Paul then moves from the incident to the theological heart of the matter: *how are people justified?* What makes someone right with God? Paul writes, "We ourselves are Jews by birth and not Gentile sinners; yet we know that a person is not justified by works of the law but through faith in Jesus Christ." These verses are the foundation of Paul's gospel. Justification—the declaration that someone is righteous in God's sight—is not achieved through human effort, law observance, or ceremonial identity markers. It rests entirely on faith in Christ. Jews and Gentiles alike must come to God on the same terms—through trust in the God who justifies the ungodly through Christ.

Paul repeats the point three different ways, not out of redundancy but to drive it deep into the hearts of the Galatians. Humans are not justified "by works of the law." They are justified "through faith in Christ." Therefore, "by works of the law no one will be justified." Paul leaves no room for negotiation. The gospel is not a cooperative effort between human effort and divine grace. It is Christ's work alone. Any system that weaves law-keeping into the foundation of justification undermines the cross.

Paul then anticipates a possible objection. Some might claim that if Jews abandon the law, they become "sinners" like Gentiles—suggesting that Christ leads them into wrongdoing. Paul rejects this idea immediately. Christ is not a servant of sin. If returning to the law is necessary for righteousness, then abandoning it is sin. But Paul insists that rebuilding the old covenant requirements would make him the transgressor—not Christ. "For through the law I died to the law," Paul says, "so that I might live to God." The law revealed sin but could not fix it. Christ accomplished what the law could not.

This leads Paul to one of the most beautiful and profound statements in the New Testament: "I have been crucified with Christ. It is no longer I who live, but Christ who lives in me." When someone trusts Christ, they are united with him in his death and resurrection. Their old identity—rooted in sin, failure, and effort—dies. A new life, shaped by Christ's presence and sustained by faith, begins. The Christian life is not a moral improvement plan. It is participation in the life of Christ himself. Paul does not live by his own strength, nor does he measure himself by the law. He lives by faith in the Son of God, who loved him and gave himself for him.

Paul concludes with a powerful warning: "If righteousness were through the law, then Christ died for no purpose." If humans could make themselves righteous by law-keeping, then the cross was unnecessary. But Christ's death is the clearest proof that salvation cannot come through human achievement. Grace stands or falls with the cross. If Christians add anything to Christ's work, they empty the cross of its meaning.

Galatians 2:11–21 weaves together story, theology, and identity. It shows that the gospel is not merely a message for conversion—it is the standard for Christian conduct. It teaches that justification is not earned through the law but received through faith. And it reveals that the Christian life is grounded in union with Christ. The gospel shapes how Christians relate to God, to one another, and to themselves. It forms communities marked by integrity, unity, and grace.

This passage invites Christians to examine their own hearts. Are there places where fear or pressure cause them to act out of step with the gospel? Are there subtle ways they create divisions that Christ has torn down? Do they live with the confidence that justification is God's gift, not their achievement? And do they embrace the profound truth that their life is now hidden with Christ, who lives in them?

Paul's confrontation with Peter is not a story of rivalry. It is a story of faithfulness. Paul loved Peter enough to defend the gospel that saved them both. And the Spirit preserved this story so Christians would see that the gospel is worth defending, worth living, and worth shaping every part of their identity.

APPLICATION

1. The gospel must shape how Christians treat one another, not just what they believe

Peter's withdrawal from the Gentile Christians shows how easy it is to affirm the gospel with our words while denying it with our actions. Peter believed Gentiles were fully accepted in Christ, yet in a moment of pressure, he acted as though their faith was incomplete. Paul calls this behavior out because the gospel is not merely a set of doctrines but a way of life. Christians today face similar temptations: social expectations, cultural norms, or personal comfort can pull them toward subtle forms of exclusion or favoritism. Whenever Christians treat others as "less than" or create divisions that Christ has already removed, they step out of line with the truth of the gospel. The message of grace calls Christians to welcome, fellowship with, and honor one another in ways that reflect Christ's work, not cultural pressure.

2. Justification by faith frees Christians from performing in order to be accepted

Paul reminds Peter—and the Galatians—that righteousness does not come from human effort but from faith in Christ. This truth is liberating. Many Christians feel the weight of trying to prove themselves to God or others. They measure their spiritual worth through busy schedules, flawless attendance, or moral achievement. While spiritual disciplines are important, they cannot earn acceptance. Paul teaches that Christians are justified because of what Christ has done, not what they accomplish. This frees Christians from anxiety-driven obedience and invites them into joyful service. When acceptance is rooted in Christ's finished work, Christians can pursue holiness out of gratitude rather than fear.

3. The Christian life is grounded in union with Christ, not self-reliance

Paul's declaration, "I have been crucified with Christ... Christ lives in me," offers a powerful picture of Christian identity. Faith is not simply believing certain truths; it is entering into a new life shaped by Christ's presence. Many Christians still try to follow Jesus by relying on their own strength, skill, or determination. But Paul teaches a different way. The Christian life is lived through Christ, who dwells within his people and empowers them to obey. This truth encourages those who feel inadequate or overwhelmed. Their strength does not come from their own limited ability, but from Christ living in them. Identity, purpose, and endurance are rooted in this union.

4. Adding requirements to the gospel empties the cross of its power

Paul ends this passage with a sober warning: if righteousness could come through the law, then Christ died for nothing. The moment Christians tie their standing before God to anything other than Christ's work, they undermine the cross. This can happen subtly—through unwritten expectations, cultural traditions, or assumptions about what "real" spirituality must look like. Paul urges Christians to resist any message that shifts the foundation from Christ's work to human effort. The cross is sufficient. Christ's death is enough. When Christians hold fast to this truth, they preserve the heart of the gospel and protect themselves from slipping back into fear-driven religion. The cross remains central, and grace remains the defining feature of the Christian life.

CONCLUSION

Galatians 2:11–21 stands at the heart of Paul's message, weaving together story, doctrine, and identity. Peter's withdrawal from Gentile Christians revealed how easily cultural pressure can distort the truth of the gospel, even among sincere followers of Jesus. Paul's confrontation was not about winning an argument or asserting authority; it was about protecting the truth that unites Christians and sustains their hope.

Justification by faith is not merely a theological statement—it is a new way of relating to God. And being crucified with Christ is not poetic language—it is a transformed identity that frees Christians from relying on their own effort. This passage reminds us that the gospel must shape everything: how Christians treat one another, how they understand themselves, and how they pursue holiness. When Christians walk in step with the truth of the gospel, the cross remains central, grace remains the foundation, and Christ remains the source of their life.

REFLECTION

1. How does Peter's withdrawal in Antioch challenge you to consider ways your actions may contradict the gospel you believe?

2. What pressures—social, cultural, or relational—tempt you to compromise the truth of the gospel in subtle ways?

3. In what areas of your life do you still struggle to trust that justification comes entirely through faith in Christ?

4. How does Paul's statement "Christ lives in me" reshape your understanding of Christian identity and daily obedience?

5. Where do you need to rely less on self-effort and more on Christ's presence and power within you?

6. How does Paul's warning about nullifying the grace of God call you to examine what you may be adding to the gospel?

DISCUSSION

1. Why did Paul confront Peter publicly instead of privately, and what does that reveal about the nature of the issue?

2. How does Peter's behavior show that even sincere Christians can act out of step with the gospel?

3. Why is justification by faith central to Paul's argument, and how does it protect the unity of the church?

4. What does it mean to be "crucified with Christ," and how does that affect a Christian's identity and priorities?

5. How does this passage help Christians discern the difference between cultural pressure and gospel truth?

6. In what ways can churches today unintentionally rebuild walls that Christ has already torn down?

5

THE BLESSING & THE CURSE

GALATIANS 3:1–14

Objective: To understand why salvation comes through faith, not law.

INTRODUCTION

In 1914, as World War I broke out across Europe, two British scientists—Sir Ernest Rutherford and Henry Moseley—were revolutionizing the field of atomic physics. Their discoveries were beginning to replace long-held theories about the structure of the atom. Yet many researchers resisted their findings because the older models had been used and trusted for decades. Some scientists found it difficult to let go of the familiar framework, even as new evidence showed a clearer and more accurate understanding of reality.

One of Moseley's key breakthroughs was the discovery that an element's identity was determined by the number of protons in its nucleus—not by its atomic weight, as previously assumed. This insight reshaped the periodic table and corrected errors that had persisted for years. When Moseley presented his findings, a colleague remarked that it felt as though "a curtain had been pulled back," transforming their understanding of atomic structure. But some chemists still clung to older models, unable or unwilling to trust the new reality, even though it explained what their theories could not.

Paul sees something similar happening in Galatians 3:1–14. The Galatians had been given a clear revelation of Christ—a picture so vivid that Paul says it was as though Jesus had been "publicly portrayed" before them. Yet they were slipping back into an older, less accurate way of relating to God: relying on the law rather than on the cross. Like scientists who returned to outdated theories despite compelling evidence, the Galatians were returning to a system that could never accomplish what Christ had already done.

In this passage, Paul urges them to remember how they received the Spirit, how Scripture presents Abraham as the model of faith, and how Christ became a curse to bring them the blessing God promised. He calls them back to the clearer, truer reality they had already seen—salvation by faith, not by works.

EXAMINATION

Galatians 3:1–14 is one of Paul's most passionate appeals in the entire letter. Up to this point he has defended the origin of his gospel and recounted his confrontation with Peter to show that justification by faith is not only true but essential for Christian fellowship. Now, Paul turns squarely toward the Galatians themselves. His tone shifts from autobiography to urgent persuasion. These Christians, whom he dearly loves, are drifting from the heart of the gospel—not because they deny Christ outright, but because they are adopting a way of relating to God that contradicts the grace they once embraced.

Paul begins with a jolt: "O foolish Galatians! Who has bewitched you?" The intensity of his words reveals the depth of his concern. He is not calling them foolish to insult them but to wake them up. Something strange has gripped their thinking—an influence that clouds their judgment and pulls them away from the truth. Paul's rhetorical question about being "bewitched" is not literal but expressive. To abandon the gospel of grace after experiencing its power is as irrational as falling under a spell. Paul wants the Galatians to see their situation with clarity before the drift becomes permanent.

He reminds them of their beginning: "It was before your eyes that Jesus Christ was publicly portrayed as crucified." Paul is not saying the Galatians personally witnessed the crucifixion but that his preaching placed the crucified Christ so clearly before them that they could almost see it. The gospel was not vague or abstract. It was Christ-centered, cross-centered, and Spirit-empowered. Their journey began with a clear vision of Jesus' sacrifice. How, then, could they turn from such a foundation to something else?

Paul then asks a series of questions aimed at restoring their memory. "Did you receive the Spirit by works of the law or by hearing with faith?" The answer is obvious. The Spirit came not through law-keeping but through faith in Christ. Paul's question is not a theological puzzle; it is a reminder of lived experience. These Christians had witnessed miracles. They had experienced the Spirit's presence, comfort, and transformation. All of it came through faith. None of it came through the law. So why, Paul asks, would they now try to mature through human effort what began through divine power? "Having begun by the Spirit, are you now being perfected by the flesh?" He knows the answer, but he wants them to hear it from their own hearts. Growth comes from the same source as salvation: the Spirit of God working through faith.

Paul now turns to Scripture—to Abraham, the father of Israel. The agitators pressuring the Galatians claimed Abraham as their model because Abraham received the covenant and circumcision. But Paul returns to an earlier moment in Abraham's story. Before he bore the covenant sign, before he performed works of obedience, Abraham "believed God, and it was counted to him as righteousness" (Gen. 15:6). Faith, not law-keeping, was the foundation of Abraham's relationship with God. Paul insists that those who share Abraham's faith—not those who share his ethnic markers—are Abraham's true children.

This is a staggering claim. The agitators argued that Gentiles needed to become culturally Jewish in order to be fully included in God's covenant family. Paul turns that argument upside down. Scripture itself declares that God's promise to bless the nations flows through faith. Abraham's story is not one of earning God's acceptance but receiving God's promise. The Galatians, as Gentiles with faith in Christ, stand in the very place Scripture predicted they would. They are "blessed along with Abraham, the man of faith." Far from being outsiders who must take on the law, they are insiders through faith alone.

Paul then contrasts this blessing with the sobering reality of relying on the law. "For all who rely on works of the law are under a curse." These words would have startled the Galatians. The law was good, holy, and a gift from God. But Paul is not belittling the law; he is showing its limitations. The law promises life to those who keep it perfectly—but none do. The law reveals the standard of righteousness, but it cannot give the power to meet that standard. Therefore, those who depend on the law for righteousness live under the weight of a curse, because the law itself says, "Cursed be everyone who does not abide by all things written in the Book of the Law, and do them."

Paul's point is not that the law is evil but that it was never designed to justify. It points to the problem but cannot solve it. This stands in contrast to faith, which brings life. "The righteous shall live by faith," Paul quotes from Habakkuk. Life comes not through striving but through trusting. The law operates on the principle of doing. Faith operates on the principle of believing. These two systems cannot be blended. They are different paths with different outcomes. To depend on the law is to take on a burden the law itself says we cannot bear. To live by faith is to receive the blessing God promised through Abraham.

At this point, Paul turns to the heart of redemption: the cross. "Christ redeemed us from the curse of the law by becoming a curse for us." These words hold the weight of the gospel. The law revealed the curse, but Christ bore the curse. The curse that humans deserved for failing to keep God's law fell on Christ instead. Paul supports his statement with Scripture: "Cursed is everyone who is hanged on a tree." Jesus took the curse so Christians could receive the blessing. In one great exchange, Christ endured the judgment that belonged to us so that we could receive the righteousness that belongs to him.

Paul then ties the entire argument together with Abraham's promise: Christ became a curse "so that in Christ Jesus the blessing of Abraham might come to the Gentiles." The promise God made to Abraham was always intended to reach the nations. The agitators wanted the Gentile Christians to become Jews in order to share Abraham's blessing. Paul says the opposite: Christ fulfilled the promise so Gentiles could receive the blessing without adopting the law. The sign of the promise is not circumcision but the Spirit. The inheritance is not tied to ethnicity but to faith. The blessing promised through Abraham reaches the world through Christ, not through the law.

As Paul steps back from his argument, the Galatians can see the contrast clearly. To return to the law is to abandon the freedom Christ purchased through his own blood. To rely on works is to step away from the Spirit who called, saved, and empowered them. To embrace Christ is to stand in the blessing God promised long before the law was given. Faith does not undermine the law; it fulfills God's purpose for the law by pointing to Christ, the one who bore its curse and brings its blessing.

Galatians 3:1–14 is not a dry theological argument. It is a pastoral plea. Paul wants these Christians to rediscover the joy of their first love—the grace that brought them into the family of God, the Spirit who filled their hearts, and the Christ who bore their curse. The law is not the problem. The problem is trying to use the law to become righteous. The gospel frees Christians from that burden by calling them to trust the one who is righteous on their behalf.

This passage invites Christians to reflect not only on their beliefs but also on their tendencies. Where do we drift toward self-reliance? Where do we forget the Spirit's role? Where do we turn obedience into a subtle attempt to earn favor? Paul's message is not that obedience is unnecessary but that obedience must flow from faith, not replace it. Christians live by trusting the God who justifies through Christ and empowers through the Spirit.

In reminding the Galatians of Abraham, Paul offers a simple yet profound picture of what faith looks like: believing God even when circumstances look impossible, trusting his promise even when the path is unclear, and receiving righteousness as a gift rather than an achievement. And in reminding them of Christ, Paul shows that the promise made to Abraham is fulfilled through the cross. The very blessing God promised the world now rests on anyone—Jew or Gentile—who places faith in the Son of God.

APPLICATION

1. The Christian life must continue in the same grace in which it began

Paul's opening question to the Galatians—"Having begun by the Spirit, are you now being perfected by the flesh?"—reveals a struggle many Christians face. It is easy to start the Christian life with dependence on God's grace and then slowly shift toward self-reliance. Spiritual routines, service, and moral disciplines become ways of measuring progress rather than expressions of gratitude. Paul reminds the Galatians that the Spirit who saved them is the Spirit who sanctifies them. Christians grow not by trying harder, but by trusting deeper—leaning on the Spirit rather than their own strength. Obedience is still essential, but it flows from grace, not from anxiety about spiritual performance. Remembering how God began his work helps Christians continue in the same posture of faith.

2. Abraham's story teaches that faith, not achievement, is the basis of God's blessing

The agitators in Galatia wanted Gentile Christians to adopt certain practices in order to share in Abraham's blessing. Paul responds by taking them back to Abraham's first encounter with God—before the covenant sign, before obedience, before any outward marker. Abraham believed God, and righteousness was credited to him. This truth is liberating. It means Christians do not earn their place in God's family through behavior or tradition. They receive it through trusting God's promise in Christ. Abraham's faith was not heroic; it was simple trust in what God said. Christians today are called to the same posture. When they respond to God with faith, they stand in the blessing God intended for all nations, without needing to prove themselves through external markers.

3. Christ bore the curse so Christians could live in freedom and blessing

One of the most profound statements in this passage is that Christ "became a curse for us." Those words reveal both the seriousness of sin and the depth of God's love. The law exposes humanity's inability to meet God's standard, placing everyone under a curse. But Christ stepped into that curse so Christians would never have to bear it. The blessing promised through Abraham flows to all nations through Christ's sacrificial death. This means Christians no longer live under fear of condemnation or under the pressure to earn righteousness. They live in the freedom Christ purchased. Remembering that Christ bore the curse leads Christians to humility, gratitude, and deeper devotion—not out of fear, but out of joy in what Christ has done.

4. Relying on human effort subtly undermines the cross and diminishes joy

Paul ends this section by contrasting the curse of the law with the blessing of faith. Whenever Christians rely on their own effort to secure God's favor, they step toward a path that cannot give life. This self-reliant mindset may appear disciplined, rigorous, or commendable, but it undermines the cross by implying that Christ's work is not enough. Paul wants Christians to see the danger not only theologically but personally. A life built on effort leads to exhaustion, comparison, and discouragement. A life built on faith leads to peace and joy. The cross frees Christians from the burden of self-effort and invites them to rest in Christ's finished work. When Christians trust in him rather than themselves, they experience the joy of walking in grace rather than striving for approval.

CONCLUSION

Galatians 3:1–14 is Paul's plea for the Galatians to return to the clarity of the gospel they first embraced. He reminds them that their lives in Christ began with the Spirit, not through human effort. Abraham's story confirms that God declares people righteous through faith, not through works. And the cross stands as the ultimate evidence that righteousness cannot come through the law—Christ bore the curse so Christians could receive the blessing.

Paul's questions, Scripture references, and vivid contrasts all point to one truth: the Christian life must rest on faith from beginning to end. When Christians rely on their own effort, they step back toward a system the law itself cannot sustain. But when they trust in Christ, they experience the freedom, blessing, and life the gospel promises. Paul's aim is not to shame the Galatians but to awaken them. The path of grace they started on is still the path God calls them to walk today.

REFLECTION

1. How does Paul's sharp tone in this section reveal the seriousness of drifting from the gospel?

2. Where do you see tendencies in your own life to begin in the Spirit but continue in self-effort?

3. How does Abraham's example challenge your assumptions about what it means to be "spiritually mature"?

4. What emotions surface when you consider that Christ became a curse for you personally?

5. Where do you feel the pull to rely on religious routines or habits as if they secure your standing with God?

6. How does remembering the Spirit's work in your life renew your trust in God's ongoing work today?

DISCUSSION

1. Why does Paul begin this section by asking, "Who has bewitched you"? What does that reveal about the Galatians' confusion?

2. How do Paul's questions about receiving the Spirit challenge any attempt to rely on the law?

3. Why is Abraham such an important figure in Paul's argument about justification by faith?

4. How does Paul explain the difference between the "curse of the law" and the "blessing of Abraham"?

5. What does it mean for Christ to "become a curse," and how does that shape Christian identity and assurance?

6. How does Galatians 3:1–14 help modern Christians discern the difference between obedience motivated by grace and obedience motivated by fear?

6

HEIRS OF THE PROMISE

GALATIANS 3:15-29

Objective: To show how God's promise, the law's purpose, and our new identity in Christ shape the Christian life.

INTRODUCTION

In 1843, a 14-year-old boy named Robert Smalls was hired as an apprentice on the docks of Charleston, South Carolina. Because he was enslaved, Smalls had no legal identity of his own. His value, in the eyes of the law, was tied entirely to the will of someone else. Yet over the next two decades, he became an expert pilot, learning every channel, sandbar, and hidden passage in Charleston Harbor. His skill was undeniable—but none of it changed his legal status. No accomplishment could grant him the freedom he longed for. His identity was fixed by a system he could not overcome.

Then, in May 1862, Smalls made a daring move. While the Confederate crew of the transport ship *Planter* slept ashore, Smalls took command, raised the appropriate signals, sailed past Confederate forts under the cover of darkness, and delivered the ship—along with its cannons, cargo, and passengers—to the Union Navy. His courage won him freedom and changed his identity forever. He was no longer property. He was recognized as a pilot in the United States Navy, later elected to Congress, and became one of the most influential African American leaders of the nineteenth century. His new identity did not come from his skill as a pilot or from years of service—it came from an act that broke the power of the system that once defined him.

Paul's message in Galatians 3:15–29 works in a similar way—but on a spiritual scale far greater. The Galatians were tempted to let the law determine their identity, their standing, and their relationship with God. But Paul reminds them that God's promise to Abraham came long before the law and was fulfilled in Christ. The law revealed their need, but it could not free them. Their identity was changed—permanently—through a decisive act of God in Christ, who fulfilled the promise and brought them into God's family.

In this passage, Paul shows that Christians are not defined by their past, their performance, or their pedigree. They are defined by Christ. They have "put on Christ" in baptism, becoming heirs of the promise and full members of God's family. Their identity is secure because it rests on God's promise, not on human effort.

EXAMINATION

Galatians 3:15–29 is one of the richest theological sections in Paul's letter, and it sits at the heart of his argument. After confronting the Galatians with the folly of leaving the path of faith, Paul now carefully builds a theological foundation to show why neither the law nor human effort can secure righteousness. This passage answers three major questions:

- What is the place of God's promise?
- What is the purpose of the law?
- And who truly belongs to God's family?

Paul answers each of these not with abstract theory but with a sweeping story of God's work in Scripture, culminating in Christ.

Paul begins with a simple illustration from everyday life. Even in human relationships, once a covenant is established, no one can come along later and change it. Contracts, wills, and agreements are binding. If this is true among people, how much more is it true of God? The promise God made to Abraham was not tentative or negotiable. It was firm, gracious, and irrevocable. God pledged to bless Abraham and all nations through him. This promise rests on God's character, not Abraham's qualifications. It is unconditional in its foundation and universal in its scope.

Paul draws attention to a detail in the promise that many would overlook: the word "offspring" is singular. Paul is not playing word games; he is showing that the promise pointed forward to one particular descendant—Christ. The blessing promised to Abraham would ultimately come through Jesus. This means the promise and the gospel belong to the same story. When God spoke to Abraham, he was already preparing the way for Christ. This turns the Galatians' whole situation upside-down. The agitators wanted Christians to root their identity in the law given centuries after Abraham, but Paul insists that Christians must root their identity in a promise that came *before* the law and is fulfilled in Christ.

Paul presses the point even further. If the inheritance depends on the law, then it no longer depends on the promise. But God gave the inheritance to Abraham by promise, not law. This means the law cannot be the foundation of the Christian life. It cannot serve as the basis of righteousness. It cannot replace the promise. The promise is the foundation; Christ is its fulfillment; and faith is the means by which Christians receive it. To act as though the law is ultimate is to misunderstand the entire story God has been telling.

Having established the priority of the promise, Paul turns to the obvious question: *Why then the law?* If the law is not the basis for righteousness, what role does it play? The agitators saw the law as essential to belonging. Paul sees it differently. "It was added because of transgressions," he says. The law entered the story to expose humanity's need, not to fix the problem. It reveals sin, restrains wrongdoing, and prepares the way for Christ, but it cannot give the life it describes.

Paul also points out that the law came through intermediaries—angels and Moses—whereas the promise came directly from God. This is not meant to diminish the law but to show that the promise has a different character. The promise is personal, direct, and rooted in God's own initiative. The law is mediated and temporary. It is part of the story but not the foundation of the story. God himself stands behind the promise, while the law serves as a guardian until Christ comes.

Paul then answers another crucial question: is the law contrary to God's promises? Absolutely not. The law is not the enemy; sin is. The law and promise do not compete with one another but serve different purposes in God's plan. If a law could have given life, then righteousness would indeed come through the law. But the law was never designed to impart life. Instead, it reveals humanity's inability to achieve righteousness on their own. Paul describes the law's effect with strong language: Scripture "imprisoned everything under sin." This is not God imprisoning people for cruelty; it is God exposing the reality of the human condition so the promise could be received by faith. The law shines a light on the problem; Christ provides the solution.

Paul now introduces one of his most vivid metaphors: the law as a "guardian," sometimes translated "schoolmaster" or "custodian." In the ancient world, a guardian was not a teacher but a strict household supervisor—often a slave—assigned to guide and discipline children until they reached maturity. The guardian's authority was real but temporary. When the child grew up, the guardian's role ended. Paul says the law served a similar role. It watched over God's people, corrected them, pointed out wrongdoing, and made clear the need for Christ. But when Christ came, the role of the guardian was fulfilled. Christians are no longer under that supervision. They have reached maturity—not because they outgrew the law morally, but because Christ has come and made them full members of God's family.

This brings Paul to his final and climactic point: identity. "For in Christ Jesus you are all sons of God through faith." Paul does not say that Christians will become God's children someday; he says they already are. The foundation is not ethnicity, law-keeping, or heritage. It is faith in Christ. This truth reshapes everything about how Christians see themselves and one another.

Paul strengthens this point by reminding the Galatians of their baptism. "For as many of you as were baptized into Christ have put on Christ." Baptism is the moment when Christians identify with Christ's death and resurrection. It symbolizes the end of the old life and the beginning of a new one. To "put on Christ" is to receive a new identity, like putting on a new garment that covers everything beneath it. This is not a change Christians achieve; it is a gift they receive. In Christ, their identity is no longer defined by their past, their failures, or their cultural background. It is defined by their union with Christ.

Paul then states one of the most radical implications of the gospel in the ancient world: "There is neither Jew nor Greek, there is neither slave nor free, there is no male and female, for you are all one in Christ Jesus." Paul is not erasing these distinctions from human experience; he is removing them as boundaries to fellowship and status in God's family. In the old world, these categories determined privilege, access, and identity. In Christ, none of them determine a person's place in God's family. The gospel dismantles all human hierarchies. Every Christian stands on equal footing because every Christian stands in Christ.

Paul ends the section by returning to Abraham: "If you are Christ's, then you are Abraham's offspring, heirs according to promise." This is the heart of Paul's argument. The Galatians do not need the law to become Abraham's children. They already are, through Christ. The blessing God promised to Abraham now belongs to them because Christ has made them heirs. Their identity is not provisional or partial. It is full, complete, and rooted in the promise God made long before the law was given.

Galatians 3:15–29 invites Christians today to marvel at the beauty of God's plan. The promise given to Abraham was never a small story about one nation; it was the beginning of God's plan to bless the world. The law was never a detour; it was a preparation. And the identity Christians receive in Christ is not fragile; it is secure, rooted in God's eternal promise and Christ's finished work.

This passage also invites self-examination. Do Christians unknowingly treat their identity as conditional, based on performance or heritage? Do they misunderstand the role of the law, either by dismissing it or by depending on it? Do they create boundaries God has already removed? Paul answers all of these with the same truth: the promise came first, the law served a temporary purpose, and in Christ Christians are full heirs of God's blessing. The story God began in Abraham finds its fulfillment and its family in Christ.

APPLICATION

1. God's promise, not human effort, is the foundation of the Christian life

Paul's contrast between the promise to Abraham and the law given at Sinai reminds Christians that their relationship with God rests on his initiative, not theirs. The Galatians were tempted to treat the law as if it were the foundation, but Paul shows that God's promise came first and remains unshakable. Christians today can fall into similar patterns—anchoring their confidence in their routines, their moral performance, or their spiritual accomplishments. But the gospel calls Christians back to the steady ground of God's faithfulness. The promise God made and fulfilled in Christ does not shift with our successes or our failures. It invites Christians to rest in a salvation that does not depend on their ability to perform but on God's unwavering commitment to bless, redeem, and adopt through Christ.

2. The law exposes need but cannot produce life, directing Christians to Christ

Paul's explanation of the law's purpose protects Christians from two common misunderstandings. Some treat the law as unnecessary because they misunderstand grace. Others treat the law as a ladder to climb toward righteousness. Paul shows that neither view captures the truth. The law is a mirror—it reveals sin, clarifies God's standards, and demonstrates the impossibility of achieving righteousness through human effort. But mirrors cannot clean what they reveal. The law prepares the heart for Christ by showing the need for him. When Christians understand this, they avoid both legalism and lawlessness. They honor the law for what it does—expose need—while clinging to Christ for what only he can do—give life. The result is humility, gratitude, and deeper faith.

3. Baptism into Christ gives Christians a new and unshakable identity

Paul's reminder that Christians "put on Christ" in baptism speaks to the longing many people have for a secure identity. In a world that often defines people by achievement, background, or status, Paul declares that Christians are defined by Christ. Baptism marks the moment when someone embraces this identity—dying to the old life and rising into a new one founded in Christ's grace. This does not erase personality or heritage, but it does replace them as sources of identity. Christians are God's children. They are clothed with Christ. They belong to a family shaped not by culture but by grace. When Christians grasp this truth, it frees them from the pressure to build their identity through approval or achievement and anchors them in the unchanging love of God.

4. The gospel creates a community of equals united in Christ

Paul's statement that there is "neither Jew nor Greek... slave nor free... male and female" is not a denial of human difference but a declaration that these differences do not determine worth or belonging in the family of God. The gospel dismantles barriers that once separated people by status, ethnicity, or gender. In Christ, all stand on equal footing as heirs of God's promise. This truth gives Christians a powerful calling: to build communities where dignity is shared, favoritism has no place, and unity is grounded in Christ alone. When Christians treat one another with equal honor, they reflect the reality of the new creation and bear witness to the world that God's promise to Abraham has truly reached the nations.

CONCLUSION

Galatians 3:15–29 draws the Galatians—and all Christians—into the larger story God has been telling since the days of Abraham. The promise came first, revealing God's determination to bless all nations through a single offspring—Christ. The law, given centuries later, served an important but temporary role. It exposed human need, clarified God's standard, and prepared the way for Christ, but it could never give life. When Christ came, he fulfilled the promise and brought God's people into maturity.

Through faith and baptism, Christians are united with Christ, clothed with him, and welcomed as full heirs of Abraham's promise. Their identity is no longer shaped by law, culture, or status, but by their union with the Son of God. Paul wants the Galatians to see that their standing before God rests not on human effort but on God's unbreakable promise. And he wants Christians today to embrace the same truth: the gospel gives a new identity rooted in Christ, secured by grace, and shared equally among all who belong to him.

REFLECTION

1. How does remembering the priority of God's promise reshape your understanding of salvation and spiritual growth?

2. Where do you see yourself relying on effort, discipline, or performance instead of resting in God's promise?

3. What emotions arise when you reflect on the law as a "guardian" that pointed you toward Christ?

4. How does baptism help anchor your identity when you feel insecure or uncertain about your worth?

5. Which human categories or distinctions are hardest for you to let go of when thinking about Christian unity?

6. What practical steps can you take to live more fully in the identity Paul describes in this passage?

DISCUSSION

1. Why does Paul emphasize that the covenant promise to Abraham cannot be annulled or adjusted by the law?

2. What does Paul mean when he says the law was "added because of transgressions"?

3. How does the metaphor of the law as a "guardian" clarify its purpose?

4. Why is baptism so central to Paul's explanation of Christian identity in this passage?

5. How does Galatians 3:28 challenge both ancient and modern divisions within the church?

6. In what ways does this passage help Christians avoid legalism on one side and license on the other?

7

FROM SLAVES TO SONS

GALATIANS 4:1-7

Objective: To celebrate the Father's adoption, the Son's redemption, and the Spirit's assurance that Christians are God's children and heirs.

INTRODUCTION

In 1990, a boy named David entered the foster care system in New Jersey after years of instability and neglect. For a long time, he bounced between temporary homes, agencies, and short-term placements. Every move reinforced the same painful message: nothing was permanent, and no one was committed to him. He had a place to sleep, but he never truly felt like he belonged.

That changed when Peter and Christine Foran, a couple who had fostered several children, met David. They noticed something immediately: David didn't unpack. He kept his few belongings in a plastic bag, ready to move again. They gently encouraged him to settle in, but years of uncertainty had taught him not to trust stability.

Over time, the Forans pursued him with patient love—attending his school events, helping with homework, involving him in family routines. Slowly, David began to believe he was more than a temporary guest. In 1993, the adoption became official. When the judge declared David legally a member of the Foran family, he later said he felt something he had never known: *security*. He belonged. He was home.

Paul describes something similar—but infinitely deeper—in Galatians 4:1-7. Christians are not temporary guests in God's house, waiting to see whether they will be allowed to stay. Through the Father's initiative, the Son's redemption, and the Spirit's assurance, Christians receive full adoption. They do not tiptoe through the Christian life wondering whether they belong. They cry, "Abba, Father," because the God who redeemed them has made them his children and heirs forever.

EXAMINATION

Galatians 4:1-7 is one of Paul's most tender and profound descriptions of what it means to belong to God. Up to this point, Paul has argued with sharp clarity that Christians are justified by faith, heirs of Abraham, and no longer under the guardianship of the law. Now he slows the pace and opens a window into the relational heart of the gospel. If Galatians 3 was about the structure of God's plan, Galatians 4 is about the warmth of God's welcome. The passage is rich with family language—sons, inheritance, adoption, Abba—revealing that the gospel is not only about being forgiven, but about being invited into God's household with the full rights of children.

Paul begins with an illustration drawn from the family structures of the ancient world. A child, even though he is the rightful heir of the entire estate, often lived no differently than a slave while he was still a minor. Even though the estate belonged to him, he had no real authority or independence. He was supervised, disciplined, and instructed by guardians until the time set by his father. Paul uses this picture to describe life under the law. Israel, though the heir of God's promises, lived under the restrictions of the law—a guardian placed over them until the time of fulfillment arrived. The law was not the enemy; it was the temporary structure God used to prepare his people for maturity.

Paul then turns from the analogy to reality: "In the same way, we also, when we were children, were enslaved to the elementary principles of the world." His words include both Jews and Gentiles. Jews were under the law; Gentiles were enslaved to idolatry and spiritual forces. Both groups were waiting for the moment when God would act decisively. Human effort could not move things forward. No ritual, tradition, or discipline could usher in maturity. That moment belonged to God alone.

And then Paul writes one of the most beautiful sentences in Scripture:

"But when the fullness of time had come, God sent forth his Son." Nothing about this timing was accidental. God did not act early. He did not act late. He acted at the precise moment he had determined, according to a plan that stretched back to Abraham and beyond. The sending of the Son was not a reaction to human failure but the fulfillment of God's promise. The Son "was born of woman," affirming his true humanity, and "born under the law," meaning he fully entered the human condition and placed himself under the very structure Israel had lived beneath. Christ did not redeem humanity from a distance; he stepped into our world, our limitations, and our obligations.

Paul states the purpose clearly: "to redeem those who were under the law, so that we might receive adoption as sons." Redemption and adoption stand side by side in this passage. Redemption frees Christians from bondage; adoption welcomes them into family. Redemption removes barriers; adoption grants belonging. Redemption pays the price of freedom; adoption grants the privilege of inheritance. Paul wants the Galatians to see that the gospel is not merely a legal transaction but a relational transformation. Christians are not pardoned criminals standing outside God's house. They are sons and daughters welcomed inside.

But Paul does not stop with the Son's work. He continues: "Because you are sons, God has sent the Spirit of his Son into our hearts, crying, 'Abba! Father!'" The Father sends the Son to accomplish redemption; the Father sends the Spirit to apply adoption. The Spirit does more than inform Christians of their new identity; he assures them of it. The cry "Abba" is not formal or distant. It is the intimate word a child would use for a loving father. Paul uses it elsewhere in Romans 8, reinforcing the theme that the Spirit's work is deeply personal. Christians do not simply know they are God's children; they experience it. The Spirit awakens love, trust, confidence, and relational closeness with God. The cry "Abba" is not forced; it is the natural expression of a heart transformed by the Spirit.

Paul ends the section with a climactic declaration: "So you are no longer a slave, but a son, and if a son, then an heir through God." Everything in this passage moves in that direction. Christians are no longer slaves to the law, to sin, or to the spiritual powers of the world. They are sons—not second-tier children, not provisional members of the household, but full heirs of God's promise. Their standing does not fluctuate with their performance. Their identity is not fragile or temporary. It rests on the work of the Father, the Son, and the Spirit.

This passage speaks to the heart of the Galatians' struggle. They had begun to think that their standing before God depended on their obedience to the law. Paul responds with a different story—one rooted in God's initiative rather than human achievement. God acted in the fullness of time. God sent his Son. God sent his Spirit. God made them heirs. The Christian life does not begin with the question "What must I do for God?" but with the truth "Look what God has done for me."

Galatians 4:1–7 also offers a corrective to distorted visions of Christian spirituality. Spiritual growth does not come from returning to law-keeping or attempting to earn deeper status with God. It comes from learning to live as children of the Father, trusting the Son, and listening to the Spirit who dwells within. Adoption, not performance, forms the foundation of the Christian life. Christians obey not to achieve acceptance but because they have already been embraced.

This passage also challenges the deep insecurities many Christians carry. Some struggle to believe that God truly welcomes them. Others fear that their failures jeopardize their standing. Still others feel distant from God and assume they have fallen out of favor. Paul offers a different picture: Christians stand not on their own merit, but on the Son's redemption and the Spirit's assurance. Their identity does not crumble under weakness because it rests on God's initiative, not their strength.

Finally, Galatians 4:1–7 invites Christians to marvel at the triune nature of salvation. The Father sends. The Son redeems. The Spirit indwells. Each person of the Godhead plays a role in drawing Christians into God's family. Salvation is not merely a transaction but a relationship shaped by the Father's love, the Son's sacrifice, and the Spirit's presence.

By the end of the passage, Paul wants the Galatians to see that their inheritance has nothing to do with law-keeping and everything to do with being united to Christ. They are heirs not because they earned it but because God gave it. They are children not because they worked their way into the family but because God adopted them. The gospel is the invitation to live in that identity—with confidence, gratitude, and a heart that cries out, "Abba, Father."

APPLICATION

1. The gospel moves Christians from slavery into full membership in God's family

Paul's illustration of a child under a guardian helps Christians recognize how easy it is to live beneath the privileges God has already given. Some Christians remain stuck in a mindset shaped by fear—fear of disappointing God, fear of judgment, fear of not measuring up spiritually. They obey as though they are still trying to earn a place at God's table rather than living as children who already belong there. Paul's message challenges this mindset directly. Christians are not spiritual servants hoping for approval; they are sons welcomed with full rights and real intimacy. This changes everything. Instead of viewing God as a distant supervisor, Christians learn to approach him as a loving Father who delights in them. Leaving behind a slave mentality frees Christians to experience joy in obedience, confidence in prayer, and rest in the assurance that their identity is secure—not because of their performance, but because of God's adoption through Christ.

2. The Father sent the Son to redeem us, not to improve us

Paul emphasizes that Christ came "in the fullness of time" to redeem, not merely refine, those under the law. Redemption is a rescue mission, not a self-improvement project. Many Christians slip into thinking that God's acceptance rises and falls with their moral progress. They work tirelessly to be worthy, hoping God will meet them halfway. But Paul reminds the Galatians—and every Christian—that Christ's mission was not to strengthen human effort but to replace it with grace. He stepped into our place, bore the burden of the law, and purchased freedom with his own life. When Christians build their confidence on Christ's redemption rather than their performance, the result is peace, gratitude, and deeper dependence on him. Instead of striving anxiously to maintain God's approval, Christians learn to rest in the truth that Christ has already secured their acceptance. Obedience becomes a response to love, not a desperate attempt to earn it.

3. The Spirit assures Christians of God's love and presence

Paul's words about the Spirit crying "Abba! Father!" are not theological decoration—they describe one of the most intimate realities of the Christian life. Many Christians believe intellectually that God loves them, yet emotionally they feel distant, uncertain, or unworthy. Paul addresses that gap by showing that the Spirit's work is not merely to instruct but to assure. The Spirit awakens in Christians an instinctive cry of trust and dependence. "Abba" is the language of a child who knows they are safe. This assurance does not come from positive thinking or emotional effort; it is the Spirit's own witness rising within a Christian's heart. When doubt, discouragement, or spiritual dryness arise, Christians are invited to lean into the Spirit who reminds them of God's unwavering love. This assurance makes prayer more personal, obedience more joyful, and suffering more bearable because Christians know they are deeply and securely loved by their Father.

4. Our identity as heirs in Christ shapes how we see ourselves and others

Paul's final declaration—that Christians are sons and heirs through God—establishes an identity that goes beyond emotion or circumstance. Many people build their sense of worth on achievements, relationships, or public approval. But identities built on fragile foundations crumble under pressure. Paul offers something better: Christians belong to God because they are united with Christ, the true Son. This identity frees them from anxiety about status, fear of failure, and pressure to impress. When Christians understand themselves as heirs, they begin viewing others differently as well. No Christian is a rival or a threat; all are members of the same family. This leads to communities marked by humility, patience, and honor. Christians serve one another not to gain advantage but because they share the same Father, the same Spirit, and the same inheritance. Identity in Christ becomes the ground for unity, compassion, and genuine Christian fellowship.

CONCLUSION

Galatians 4:1–7 stands as one of Paul's clearest and warmest summaries of what God has done for his people. The passage lifts Christians out of the mindset of slavery—fear-driven obedience, spiritual insecurity, and the constant pressure to prove themselves—and places them into the family room of God. The Father sent his Son at just the right time, not to enhance the law but to redeem those under it. Through Christ's work, Christians are adopted as sons with full rights in the family. And to make that truth more than a doctrine, the Father sends the Spirit, who teaches Christians to cry out with confidence, "Abba, Father."

Paul wants the Galatians to see that their identity does not rest in the law, their ancestry, or their performance. It rests in the heart of God, expressed through the work of the Son and sealed by the Spirit. Christians are no longer slaves. They are sons and heirs, welcomed forever into God's family.

REFLECTION

1. How does Paul's image of moving from slavery to sonship challenge the way you relate to God on a daily basis?

2. Where do you still sense traces of a "slave mentality"—fear, insecurity, or the need to prove yourself spiritually?

3. How does remembering the Father's timing in sending the Son strengthen your trust in God's sovereignty and care?

4. In what ways have you experienced the Spirit prompting the cry of "Abba, Father" in your own heart?

5. How does your identity as an adopted child of God reshape the way you see your worth, purpose, and future?

6. What relationships in your life could be transformed by remembering that every Christian is a full heir in God's family?

DISCUSSION

1. Why does Paul compare life under the law to the experience of a child under a guardian? What does this reveal about spiritual maturity?

2. How do the Father's sending of the Son and the Spirit work together to secure the Christian's identity and assurance?

3. What does Paul mean when he says Christians are "no longer slaves but sons"? How is this different from simply being forgiven?

4. How does the Spirit's cry of "Abba, Father" help Christians understand and experience their relationship with God?

5. Why is the concept of adoption crucial for understanding the gospel, and how does it correct misunderstandings about performance-based faith?

6. How does this passage shape the way Christians should treat one another within the church? What divisions does it challenge?

8

UNTIL CHRIST IS FORMED IN YOU

GALATIANS 4:8-20

Objective: To expose false motives and warn against spiritual slavery.

INTRODUCTION

In 1907, a young doctor named William James Mayo stood before a group of graduating medical students in Chicago. He warned them about a danger they would face throughout their careers—not disease, but misleading admiration. He explained that patients often praised their physicians excessively, placing blind trust in them simply because they felt cared for or impressed by their manner. Mayo urged the students to guard their integrity fiercely, reminding them that "the safest thing is the truth," even when truth is difficult, unpopular, or unwelcome.

A few years later, during a typhoid outbreak in Minnesota, Mayo's words proved prophetic. Some community leaders began promoting untested treatments and comforting—but false—assurances. Crowds flocked to these voices because they offered hope wrapped in charm. But the Mayo brothers chose a different path. They confronted misinformation directly, even when people grew frustrated with their blunt honesty. Their commitment to truth saved lives, though it cost them popularity in the moment.

Paul's tone in Galatians 4:8-20 carries that same weight of responsibility. The Galatians were drawn toward teachers who "made much of them"—whose flattery felt comforting and whose rules seemed reassuring. But Paul loved them too much to stay silent. He tells them the truth plainly, even at the risk of losing their affection. He reminds them of the freedom they once embraced, the joy they once knew, and the relationship they once shared. He warns them of the danger of returning to spiritual slavery and pleads for Christ to be formed in them again.

This passage shows the heart of a true shepherd—one who speaks honestly, loves deeply, and longs for the spiritual good of those he serves, even when the truth is costly.

EXAMINATION

Galatians 4:8–20 is one of the most personal and emotional parts of Paul's letter. After giving rich theological arguments about justification, adoption, and identity, Paul shifts into the language of longing, pain, and urgency. The tone changes. He is not merely defending doctrine; he is pleading with people he loves. In this section, Paul's pastoral heart is on full display. He is not speaking as an academic, an administrator, or a theologian detached from emotion. He is speaking as a spiritual father watching his children drift toward danger.

Paul begins by reminding the Galatians of their former life: "Formerly, when you did not know God, you were enslaved to those that by nature are not gods." Before coming to Christ, the Galatians lived in idolatry. They served false gods—images, rituals, spiritual forces, and cultural expectations that held them captive. Their daily lives were shaped by fear and superstition. They tried to earn favor, appease spirits, and maintain their place in the social and religious system. Paul calls that condition slavery. It was bondage wrapped in religion.

But after hearing the gospel, everything changed. "Now that you have come to know God, or rather to be known by God…" Paul corrects himself because the greater miracle is not that they recognized God but that God recognized them. The God of creation noticed them, pursued them, and claimed them as his own. This relationship was not built on their initiative but on God's grace. Knowing God and being known by him were the marks of their new life—marks far greater than any religious ritual.

Paul then asks one of the most heartbreaking questions in the letter: "How can you turn back again to the weak and worthless elementary principles of the world?" The Galatians were not returning to pagan idols;

they were returning to the Jewish law. But Paul sees no real difference. Whether it is the pagan calendar or the Jewish calendar, whether it is Gentile rituals or Jewish rituals, the principle is the same: people trying to earn their place with God through religious performance. That is what Paul calls slavery. The problem is not the form of the ritual but the function it plays. Anything that replaces Christ as the basis of belonging becomes an idol— even if it comes from Scripture.

Paul mentions their renewed attention to "days and months and seasons and years," showing how these observances had become markers of spiritual status. The Galatians were slipping into a mindset where ritual compliance felt safer than simple faith. Paul fears that his labor among them might have been "in vain"—not because he doubts the gospel but because he sees them abandoning it in practice. His fear is not frustration but parental worry. Parents know what it is like to watch a child walk into danger and feel powerless to stop it.

At this point, Paul shifts his tone. His concern becomes personal. "Brothers, I entreat you, become as I am, for I also have become as you are." This is not arrogance. Paul is appealing to the shared life they once enjoyed. He had lived among them not as a distant Jewish teacher but as one of them—a man who embraced the freedoms of the gospel in their presence. He asks them to return to the same freedom because they had stopped living as equals in the household of God.

He reminds them of the warmth they once showed him. When he first preached to them, he did so "because of a bodily ailment," which suggests Paul was unexpectedly delayed in Galatia due to sickness. Instead of seeing his illness as a burden, the Galatians welcomed him with extraordinary kindness. They did not despise him or reject him. They received him "as an angel of God" and even "as Christ Jesus." Their affection had been so deep that Paul says they would have "gouged out [their] eyes and given them to [him]." This level of devotion shows how powerfully the gospel had impacted their hearts at the beginning.

But now things have changed. "Have I then become your enemy by telling you the truth?" Paul's question reveals the emotional distance that had formed. He had not changed his message, but the Galatians' loyalties had changed. The false teachers—whom Paul simply calls "they"—had won their attention by using flattery and manipulation. "They make much of you, but for no good purpose." These teachers were zealous, persuasive, and seemingly devoted, but their goal was not the Galatians' wellbeing. Paul says they wanted to "shut you out," meaning they wanted to isolate the Galatians from Paul so they could control them.

This manipulation is subtle but powerful. The false teachers used attention, affirmation, and exclusivity to pull the Galatians away from grace. Paul warns that zeal alone is not a mark of spiritual maturity. What matters is whether that zeal is directed toward good. The false teachers were zealous, but their zeal led to bondage. Paul's zeal led to freedom.

Paul then uses one of the most intimate descriptions in his letters: "My little children, for whom I am again in the anguish of childbirth until Christ is formed in you!" The metaphor of childbirth emphasizes Paul's pain, persistence, and personal investment. He had labored once already when he first preached the gospel to them. Now he feels as though he must labor again because the Galatians were slipping back into spiritual immaturity. Paul is not angry; he is heartbroken. His deepest desire is not to win an argument but to see Christ fully formed in their lives.

The phrase "Christ formed in you" reveals Paul's vision for Christian maturity. The goal of the Christian life is not behavioral compliance or impressive knowledge. It is becoming like Christ in character, faith, love, humility, and trust. Everything Paul says in this passage flows from that central desire. He wants the Galatians to live in the freedom Christ purchased, to experience the love of the Father, to walk in the assurance of the Spirit, and to reflect the character of Christ.

Paul ends this section by confessing his perplexity. "I wish I could be present with you now and change my tone, for I am perplexed about you." These words show the tension of pastoral ministry. He does not want to be harsh. He does not want to speak through letters when his presence would offer comfort, correction, and clarity. But until he can be with them, he writes with urgency. His perplexity is the confusion of a minister who cannot understand how those he loves could drift so quickly from grace.

Galatians 4:8–20 offers a vivid reminder that theology and pastoral love cannot be separated. Paul argues passionately for the truth of the gospel because he loves the people who are drifting from it. His warnings come from concern, not superiority. His rebukes come from affection, not anger. And his longing comes from a deep desire to see Christ formed in them.

This passage also reveals how Christians are vulnerable to spiritual drift. It does not begin with open rejection but with subtle substitutions—

ritual replacing trust, flattery replacing truth, zeal replacing discernment. Paul calls Christians to remember their first love, to examine their loyalties, and to hold fast to the freedom Christ has given them.

Ultimately, Galatians 4:8–20 shows that the gospel is not merely a message to believe but a relationship to live. God knows his people. Christ redeemed them. The Spirit dwells within them. And shepherds, teachers, and fellow Christians labor with love so that Christ may be formed in the community of faith.

APPLICATION

1. Beware of the slow drift back toward spiritual slavery

Paul fears that the Galatians are returning to "the weak and worthless elementary principles" they once escaped. Their drift is not dramatic; it is subtle. They are adopting practices that make them feel safe, spiritual, and disciplined, yet those practices undermine the gospel by shifting trust from Christ to ritual. Christians today face the same temptation. It is easy to slide from grace into performance—trusting routines, rules, or traditions to secure God's favor. This mindset feels comfortable because it offers a sense of control, but it leads back to slavery. Paul calls Christians to examine the quiet ways in which they rely on anything other than Christ. The gospel invites Christians to live as people who are known by God—not people who are trying to earn his attention. Returning to slavery is not only unnecessary; it is tragic for those who have already been welcomed into God's family.

2. Spiritual flattery is dangerous because it appeals to pride rather than truth

Paul exposes the manipulative strategy of the false teachers: "They make much of you, but for no good purpose." Their method was not open hostility but strategic flattery. They offered attention, exclusivity, and approval in exchange for loyalty. Christians today still face spiritual leaders or voices who use charm and affirmation to gain influence. Flattery feels encouraging, but it easily becomes a trap. When Christians begin to crave approval from people rather than security in Christ, they lose discernment. Paul teaches that genuine spiritual leadership aims for Christ to be formed in people—not to win followers or build personal platforms. Christians must learn to distinguish between voices that feed pride and voices that promote truth. The gospel produces humility, not dependence on human approval. Flattery distracts; the gospel frees.

3. Painful truth-telling is part of genuine Christian love

Paul asks, "Have I become your enemy by telling you the truth?" This question reveals something deeply important: love sometimes requires saying things people do not want to hear. The Galatians once welcomed Paul as if he were an angel from God, but now they resent the very person who brought them the gospel. Christians often react similarly. When someone lovingly confronts them about unhealthy patterns, misplaced trust, or spiritual drift, the first instinct is defensiveness. Yet Paul models a love that refuses to stay silent. True Christian friendship and leadership involve telling the truth gently but firmly, even when it risks misunderstanding. Christians must cultivate hearts willing to receive loving correction. The goal is never to wound but to heal—to protect the freedom Christ provides and to prevent hidden dangers from taking root. Loving truth-telling is a mark of deep, Christ-shaped community.

4. Christlikeness is the goal of Christian ministry

Paul describes his longing using the language of childbirth: "I am again in the anguish of childbirth until Christ is formed in you." His goal is not to win arguments, gather followers, or secure influence. It is to see Christ formed in the lives of believers. This is the measure of faithful ministry. The same must be true for Christians today. Whether as teachers, parents, mentors, or friends, the aim is not to create dependence, establish superiority, or impress others. It is to help one another grow into the likeness of Christ. This perspective reorients how Christians serve. It brings patience, because spiritual formation takes time. It brings humility, because only God can truly change the heart. And it brings love, because Christians labor not for personal gain but for the growth of others. When Christ is the goal, ministry remains grounded in grace.

CONCLUSION

Galatians 4:8–20 reveals the deep, emotional heartbeat of Paul's ministry. He is not defending the gospel from a distance; he is pleading with people he loves. The Galatians had once embraced freedom with joy, but their drift toward laws, rituals, and flattery threatened to pull them back into a form of slavery. Paul reminds them that the Christian life is not built on performance or approval but on being known by God. He exposes the manipulative motives of the false teachers, not to shame the Galatians but to protect them. And he speaks as a spiritual father who longs to see Christ fully formed in them, even if it means expressing concern, frustration, and anguish.

This passage shows that faithful ministry is rooted in truth and love. It challenges Christians to remain anchored in grace, to discern the voices they follow, and to welcome the kind of loving correction that guards the heart and strengthens faith. Paul's plea still echoes today: stay in the freedom Christ has given you, and let his life be formed in yours.

REFLECTION

1. How do you see subtle forms of spiritual slavery trying to creep back into your walk with God?

2. What comforts or routines tempt you to rely on performance rather than resting in God's grace?

3. Whose approval do you tend to seek, and how does that shape the way you respond to truth?

4. How has someone's honest correction helped you grow in your relationship with Christ?

5. What does Paul's anguish for the Galatians teach you about the heart of genuine Christian ministry?

6. Where do you most need Christ to be "formed in you" right now?

DISCUSSION

1. Why does Paul say returning to religious rituals is no different than returning to pagan slavery?

2. How does Paul's statement that the Galatians were "known by God" deepen your understanding of grace?

3. What does the Galatians' former affection for Paul reveal about the power of the gospel to create genuine relationships?

4. Why are the motives of the false teachers so dangerous for the Galatians—and for Christians today?

5. How does Paul's metaphor of childbirth help you understand the cost and love involved in ministry?

6. What does this passage teach about the relationship between truth, love, and spiritual formation?

9

BORN OF PROMISE, NOT PERFORMANCE

GALATIANS 4:21–31

Objective: To show that Christians are children of the promise and call them to live in the freedom God gives through Christ.

INTRODUCTION

In 1849, gold fever swept across the United States as thousands of prospectors rushed westward to California. People abandoned jobs, farms, and families because they believed the promise of gold would change everything. But because most travelers didn't know the terrain, they depended on guidebooks written by adventurers who claimed to have mapped reliable shortcuts. One such book—*The Emigrant's Guide to the West*—promised a "new and faster route" across the Great Basin. The author assured travelers that this path would save weeks of hardship.

A large group of families, including the now-famous Donners, trusted that promise. But the shortcut wasn't real. It led them into some of the harshest desert in North America, costing them precious supplies, precious time, and in some cases, their lives. They followed a promise based on human speculation rather than on reality. And the more they committed to the route, the harder it became to turn back.

Paul sees the Galatians in a similar situation. They were trusting a path that promised spiritual improvement but actually led into bondage.

The false teachers insisted that returning to the law would speed their spiritual growth. It felt disciplined, respectable, and familiar—like a well-publicized "shortcut" to maturity. But Paul warns that this path, grounded in human effort, is nothing more than the road of Hagar: a route that cannot reach the destination God promised.

In Galatians 4:21–31, Paul takes the familiar story of Abraham's two sons and uses it to expose the danger of these human-made shortcuts. Freedom doesn't come from self-reliance, religious performance, or cultural identity markers. It comes only through God's promise fulfilled in Christ. Christians are Isaacs—children born not through effort but through grace.

EXAMINATION

Galatians 4:21–31 is the most daring and unexpected argument Paul makes in the entire letter. Up to this point, he has defended justification by faith, exposed the folly of returning to the law, explained the purpose of the law in God's plan, and described the beauty of adoption through Christ. Now he turns to the story of Abraham, not simply as history but as a mirror in which the Galatians—and all Christians—can see the danger of relying on human effort.

Paul opens with a pointed question: "Tell me, you who desire to be under the law, do you not listen to the law?" He is speaking to those who think the Mosaic law—its rituals, markers, and identity-shaping customs—will make them better Christians. These Galatians, influenced by the false teachers, believe that adding law observance will bring spiritual maturity. Paul places a challenge before them: if they truly want the law, then they must listen to what the law actually says.

He then recounts the story of Abraham's two sons. This story was well known to Jews and Gentiles alike. Abraham fathered Ishmael through Hagar and Isaac through Sarah. But for Paul, the key point is not biological but theological: "One was born according to the flesh, the other through promise." Ishmael's birth resulted from human planning, anxiety, and effort. Abraham and Sarah attempted to produce God's promise on their own by following customary ancient Near Eastern practices. They engineered a solution because they doubted God's timing. Isaac's birth, on the other hand, came through divine intervention. He arrived in humanly impossible circumstances—Sarah was long past childbearing age—and his birth was the direct fulfillment of God's promise.

Paul uses these two births as symbols of two ways of approaching God. Ishmael represents human effort—people trying to achieve God's blessing through their own strategies. Isaac represents divine promise— God accomplishing what humans cannot. Throughout the letter, Paul has emphasized that righteousness, adoption, identity, and blessing come through God's promise in Christ, not through obedience to the law. Here, he anchors that truth in the story of Abraham's household.

Paul then makes a bold move: he says Hagar represents Mount Sinai, the covenant of law, and "the present Jerusalem." This would have shocked his readers. Many Jewish believers assumed that the law—and Jerusalem as its center—represented spiritual superiority. But Paul reverses the categories. Because the law brings condemnation rather than righteousness, those who rely on the law are like Ishmael—children "born according to the flesh," bound to slavery. The "present Jerusalem," which still clings to the law, remains enslaved. Paul's language is emotionally charged, because he is speaking of a beloved but spiritually misguided people.

By contrast, Sarah represents "the Jerusalem above," the heavenly reality that supersedes earthly boundaries. This Jerusalem is free. It is the home of Christians—Jews and Gentiles alike—who have received God's promise through Christ. It is not built on law but on grace. It is not limited to ethnic Israel but extends to all nations. This heavenly Jerusalem is the mother of all who live by faith. Paul uses Isaiah 54:1 to reinforce this point: "Rejoice, O barren one who does not bear." Isaiah spoke to exiled Israel, promising that God would restore and expand his people beyond anything they imagined. Paul sees this fulfilled in the gospel, where the seemingly barren promise produces an international family through God's power.

Paul then applies the picture directly: "Now you, brothers, like Isaac, are children of promise." This statement is meant to instill confidence. The Galatians do not need the law to complete them. They do not need circumcision to validate their identity. They already belong to God because they were born not through human effort but through divine promise. Their faith in Christ has placed them in the line of Isaac, not Ishmael.

But Paul is not finished. He introduces another difficult parallel: "Just as at that time he who was born according to the flesh persecuted him who was born according to the Spirit, so it is now." The story of Ishmael mocking Isaac becomes a symbol of tension between human-effort religion and grace-based faith. Paul warns the Galatians that the false teachers—

children of the flesh—are persecuting them by insisting that law-keeping is necessary for belonging. This pressure is not a sign of spiritual progress but a sign of spiritual danger.

Paul then quotes Sarah's words from Genesis 21:10: "Cast out the slave woman and her son." In Genesis, this expulsion was about inheritance—it ensured that Isaac alone received the covenant promise. Paul uses the story as a metaphor: the Galatians must decisively reject the legalistic teaching that threatens their identity. The voice of the false teachers cannot coexist with the gospel of grace. Law and promise cannot sit side by side as equal paths to God. Just as Ishmael could not inherit alongside Isaac, legalism cannot inherit alongside Christ.

Paul concludes with a powerful reminder: "We are not children of the slave but of the free woman." For Paul, this is not poetry—it is the core of Christian identity. Christians are not spiritual Ishmaels, produced by human effort. They are spiritual Isaacs, born through God's promise. Everything about their salvation—redemption, adoption, justification, inheritance—comes through God's work in Christ, not through law-keeping.

Galatians 4:21–31 confronts Christians with two starkly different ways of relating to God. One is grounded in human effort, religious achievement, and confidence in personal performance. The other is grounded in God's grace, God's power, and God's promise. Paul is clear: only one of these paths leads to life. Only one produces freedom. Only one makes us true children of Abraham. The other leads back to bondage.

This passage challenges every generation of Christians to consider where they place their trust. Do we depend on religious routines, traditions, or moral success? Or do we rest in the finished work of Christ? The gospel insists that freedom cannot be earned; it can only be received. Grace does not merely improve human effort; it replaces it. The law reveals the problem, but only the promise provides the solution.

Paul's use of Genesis also shows that Scripture's story is ultimately a story of grace. The promise given to Abraham was never about human ingenuity. It was about God bringing life where life seemed impossible. Isaac's birth was a miracle. Christ's coming was a miracle. And the new birth of every Christian is a miracle. Faith does not create God's promise—it receives it.

But this passage also carries a warning. The pull of performance-based religion never disappears. The temptation to return to the familiar structure of rules, rituals, or identity markers remains strong. Legalism feels safe because it gives humans control. Grace feels risky because it requires trust. Paul calls Christians to choose promise over performance, freedom over slavery, and Christ over self.

Galatians 4:21–31 ultimately invites Christians to see themselves as part of the story God has been telling since Abraham. Like Isaac, they are children born not through their own effort but through God's promise. Like Abraham, they are called to trust God even when his path seems unexpected. Like Sarah, they witness God bringing life out of barrenness. And like Paul, they must "cast out" every voice that pulls them away from the freedom Christ purchased.

In Christ, Christians belong to the Jerusalem above. They are free. They are heirs. They are children of promise.

APPLICATION

1. God's promise—not human effort—is the foundation of Christian freedom

Paul uses the story of Hagar and Sarah to show that two radically different ways of relating to God exist: one grounded in human effort, the other rooted in divine promise. Ishmael symbolizes what humans can produce through planning, striving, and religious confidence. Isaac symbolizes what only God can produce through grace. Many Christians still drift toward an "Ishmael mindset"—thinking God's acceptance rests on personal performance, spiritual routines, or adherence to familiar structures. Paul insists that such thinking leads back to slavery. Freedom comes only from receiving what God has done in Christ, not from attempting to supplement it. This truth invites Christians to examine where they have substituted effort for trust. When Christians anchor themselves in God's promise rather than in their own ability, they live with deeper assurance, gratitude, and joy. Their confidence rests not in their success, but in God's faithfulness.

2. Performance-based religion always persecutes grace—even today

Paul notes that Ishmael "persecuted" Isaac, and he draws a sobering parallel: wherever human-effort religion thrives, it pressures, shames, or marginalizes those who live by grace. Christians who rest in Christ's finished work often find themselves misunderstood by those who prefer strict rules or external measures of spirituality. Legalism appears disciplined, serious, and committed, yet it quietly undermines the heart of the gospel by turning God's blessing into something earned. Paul wants Christians to be aware of this tension—not to become defensive, but to remain anchored in the gospel. When pressure arises to conform to systems that claim to offer a "better" or "safer" path to God, Christians must remember that grace is not the easy way; it is the only way. Holding to grace sometimes invites criticism, but it also brings the freedom and peace that only Christ can provide.

3. Christians must cast out every voice that undermines their identity in Christ

Paul's use of Sarah's command—"Cast out the slave woman and her son"—may strike modern readers as harsh, but he applies it spiritually, not socially. He is urging Christians to decisively reject teachings, expectations, or habits that threaten to pull them back into slavery. Many believers carry voices from their past—messages of unworthiness, pressure to perform, fear of failure, or assumptions that God's approval must be maintained through behavior. Others face present pressures from communities or leaders who elevate ritual or tradition above Christ. Paul says such voices cannot be tolerated because they oppose the gospel. Christians are called to "cast out" anything that competes with Christ as the source of identity. This act is not about arrogance but about clarity. Removing those false voices makes room for the truth: Christians are children of the promise, fully accepted because of Christ's work.

4. Christian identity is shaped by the "Jerusalem above"

Paul's contrast between the present Jerusalem and the Jerusalem above reminds Christians that their primary citizenship is heavenly, not earthly. Spiritual identity is not defined by ethnicity, culture, tradition, or denominational background. These elements may shape a person's story but cannot determine their standing before God. Christians belong to the heavenly Jerusalem—a community created by God's promise, centered on Christ, and expanded by the Spirit. Recognizing this identity changes how Christians view themselves and others. It dismantles pride, removes comparison, and undermines spiritual hierarchies. It guards Christians from elevating customs or systems to a place God never assigned them. And it cultivates humility, unity, and grace within the church. When Christians live as children of the Jerusalem above, they reflect the freedom Christ purchased and the promise God fulfilled—a freedom rooted in belonging to God, not in belonging to human categories.

CONCLUSION

Galatians 4:21–31 invites Christians to look closely at the story of Abraham's two sons and see their own spiritual lives reflected in it. Ishmael represents the human impulse to take control—to secure God's blessing through effort, ritual, or self-reliance. Isaac represents the miracle of God's promise—life produced not by human ability but by God's gracious intervention. Paul wants the Galatians to understand that returning to the law is like choosing the path of Hagar: a route that cannot produce the inheritance God has promised.

Christians are children of the free woman, not the slave; born of God's promise, not of human striving. Their identity is shaped by the Jerusalem above, not by earthly systems. And because they are children of the promise, they are free—free from the pressure to perform, free from the weight of the law, and free to live as heirs through Christ. Paul's message is both a warning and a reassurance: abandon every voice that leads back to slavery, and embrace fully the freedom God gives in his Son.

REFLECTION

1. How does the contrast between Ishmael and Isaac help you evaluate whether you relate to God through effort or through promise?

2. Where do you sense the subtle pull of performance-based religion trying to shape your spiritual identity?

3. Which "voices" in your life most often undermine your confidence in God's grace?

4. How does Paul's description of the "Jerusalem above" expand your understanding of Christian identity and belonging?

5. Where do you experience tension or criticism because you choose to rely on grace rather than religious performance?

6. How does seeing yourself as a child of promise reshape your confidence, worship, and daily walk with God?

DISCUSSION

1. Why does Paul challenge those who "desire to be under the law" to actually listen to what the law teaches?

2. What makes Ishmael's birth a picture of human effort, and Isaac's a picture of God's promise?

3. Why does Paul associate the present Jerusalem with slavery? What does that reveal about the limitations of the law?

4. How does the persecution of the child of promise illustrate the ongoing conflict between legalism and grace?

5. What does it mean to "cast out" the slave woman and her son in the context of gospel identity?

6. How does this passage shape the way Christians understand their freedom, their identity, and their place in God's family?

10

STAND FIRM IN FREEDOM
GALATIANS 5:1-12

Objective: To urge Christians to guard their freedom, reject law-based righteousness, and trust the Spirit's work in producing faith that expresses itself through love.

INTRODUCTION

In 1884, a young engineer named Washington Roebling faced an unexpected challenge. He had taken over the construction of the Brooklyn Bridge after his father's death, but a tragic accident left him bedridden, unable to return to the construction site. For months, rumors spread that the project was doomed. Some critics insisted the bridge could never be completed without Roebling's constant supervision. Others claimed the design was flawed and that safety could only be guaranteed if the plans were altered. Pressure mounted for Roebling to surrender control and allow others to "correct" the work.

But Roebling refused to abandon the original design. From his room, he communicated with the construction crew through his wife, Emily, who relayed every calculation and instruction. Though cut off from the worksite, Roebling was determined to finish the bridge as it was meant to stand. The greatest danger was not the weather, the river, or the engineering—it was the pressure to abandon the proven plan for something that looked safer but would have compromised the entire structure.

Paul sees something similar happening in Galatians 5:1–12. The Galatians were being pressured to "adjust" the gospel—adding a small requirement here, a ritual there—in the name of safety, certainty, and spiritual improvement. But any adjustment to the gospel, no matter how small, threatens the integrity of the entire structure. Paul warns them that returning to the law is not a minor modification but a surrender of the freedom Christ purchased.

Just as Roebling held firmly to the original design despite pressure to alter it, Paul calls Christians to stand firm in the freedom of the gospel and refuse every voice that seeks to add to what Christ has already accomplished.

EXAMINATION

Galatians 5 marks a decisive shift in Paul's letter. After arguing fiercely that Christians are justified by faith and adopted as God's children, Paul now turns to the practical and pastoral impact of that truth. Galatians 5:1–12 is a hinge passage—looking back at everything Paul has said about grace and looking forward to the life that flows from it. Every word is charged with urgency. Paul senses the spiritual danger the Galatians face, and he refuses to soften his tone. Freedom is at stake. Identity is at stake. The gospel itself is at stake.

Paul begins with one of the most memorable sentences in the letter: "For freedom Christ has set us free." This is not sentimental language; it is a theological declaration. Christ did not redeem Christians merely to improve them, refine them, or redirect them. He redeemed them *to free them.* Freedom is not a minor theme of the gospel—it is its very essence. Freedom from guilt, freedom from the curse of the law, freedom from slavery to sin, freedom from the fear of judgment, freedom from earning acceptance—Paul insists that this is the life Christ purchased.

Because freedom is the goal, Paul immediately follows with the command: "Stand firm therefore, and do not submit again to a yoke of slavery." Christian freedom is precious, but it must be defended. The freedom Paul describes is not fragile, but Christians can be persuaded to live as though they are still slaves, even after being set free. The Galatians were drifting back toward a mindset dominated by rules, rituals, and the illusion of earning righteousness. Paul sees this not as spiritual maturity but as spiritual regression. The yoke of the law was never designed to give life. Christ removed that yoke—not so Christians could be lawless, but so they could walk in the freedom of faith empowered by the Spirit.

Paul then zeroes in on the specific issue troubling the Galatians: circumcision. "If you accept circumcision, Christ will be of no advantage to you." This is not because circumcision is inherently sinful. Paul circumcised Timothy in Acts 16 for the sake of ministry among Jews. The issue is *why* the Galatians were considering it. They were being persuaded that circumcision was a requirement for full belonging in the family of God. It had become a symbol of trust in the law rather than trust in Christ. To accept circumcision on those terms would be to shift reliance away from Jesus and toward human effort.

Paul presses the point further: "Every man who accepts circumcision is obligated to keep the whole law." The false teachers were trying to add one small requirement, but Paul exposes the flaw. The law is not a buffet where one chooses a few bite-sized obligations. To enter the law as the basis of righteousness is to enter all of it: sacrifices, food laws, purity regulations, civic codes, and covenant markers. Law-keeping is an all-or-nothing system, and it demands perfection. Paul makes clear that adding one legal requirement as a basis of righteousness is not adding "a little law." It is exchanging grace for a system that cannot save.

Then Paul delivers one of his strongest warnings: "You are severed from Christ, you who would be justified by the law; you have fallen away from grace." This is not about losing salvation as much as abandoning the path of grace. To be "severed from Christ" means to cut oneself off from Christ as the source of righteousness and to turn instead to the law. The Galatians were not merely adopting a new tradition—they were abandoning the only foundation that gives life. Paul's language is intentionally shocking because the stakes are enormous. Grace and law cannot share the same throne. Either Christ justifies, or the law does. There is no middle ground.

After this sharp warning, Paul shifts to a calmer tone, reminding the Galatians what true Christian hope looks like. "For through the Spirit, by faith, we ourselves eagerly wait for the hope of righteousness." The contrast with law is striking. The law demands action to achieve righteousness; the Spirit produces hope. The law demands proof; faith produces expectation.

Christians do not anxiously labor to secure righteousness—they wait eagerly, trusting that God will complete what he began. The Spirit's presence assures them that righteousness is coming—not because of their achievement but because of God's promise.

Then Paul summarizes the entire Christian life in one profound statement: "For in Christ Jesus neither circumcision nor uncircumcision counts for anything, but only faith working through love." External markers—whether traditional or progressive, strict or relaxed—do not define what it means to belong to Christ. What matters is faith expressing itself through love. This is the kind of obedience grace produces: not ritualistic conformity, but Spirit-driven love that reflects the character of Christ. Circumcision and uncircumcision both fall away as identity markers; love, shaped by faith, becomes the new way of life.

Paul then returns to the danger facing the Galatians. "You were running well. Who hindered you from obeying the truth?" The imagery of a race highlights their former momentum. They had begun the Christian life with clarity, passion, and joy. But now someone had stepped in front of them, tripping them up and redirecting their course. Paul makes clear that this influence "is not from him who calls you." False teaching does not originate in Christ. Its persuasive charm, its strategic appeal, and its religious discipline may seem impressive, but it never comes from the God who calls people into freedom.

He then adds a warning: "A little leaven leavens the whole lump." The false teachers were spreading a small idea—just one change, one ritual, one requirement. But Paul knows that legalism grows rapidly. One requirement becomes two. Two become ten. Soon the Christian life becomes defined by rules rather than by Christ. A small shift in reliance leads to a major shift in identity. Paul wants the Galatians to see the danger before they are swallowed by it.

Paul expresses confidence—"I have confidence in the Lord that you will take no other view"—but he also issues a severe warning to the false teachers. "The one who is troubling you will bear the penalty." He does not tolerate those who distort the gospel. Their teaching is not harmless; it is spiritually destructive. It leads people away from grace and brings them under a curse. Paul will not soften his words because he sees the harm their message causes.

Then Paul addresses an accusation the false teachers had likely made against him: that he still preached circumcision. "If I still preach circumcision, why am I still being persecuted?" If Paul were advocating circumcision as they suggested, the offense of the cross would disappear. The cross offends because it declares that human effort contributes nothing to salvation. It shatters spiritual pride. It leaves no room for boasting. To preach circumcision would remove the scandal of the cross—but it would also remove the gospel itself.

Finally, Paul ends with one of the most shocking statements in all of his letters: "I wish those who unsettle you would emasculate themselves." This is not crude anger but righteous indignation. The false teachers had turned circumcision into a mark of spiritual superiority. Paul exposes the absurdity of their logic by following it to its ultimate conclusion. If a small cut brings righteousness, why not go further? His words are forceful because the threat is serious. When people distort the gospel, Paul responds with fierce protection for those under his care.

Galatians 5:1–12 is both a pastoral plea and a theological warning. Freedom is a gift Christ purchased with his own blood. Christians do not drift into slavery all at once—they slide into it gradually by seeking identity, assurance, or spiritual confidence in anything other than Christ. Paul calls the Galatians to stand firm, to discern which voices they follow, and to guard the gospel with vigilance.

Yet the passage is not dominated by anger. Underneath Paul's urgency is a deep desire for the Galatians to experience the life God intends—the life of the Spirit, the life of hope, the life characterized by faith working through love. Law-based righteousness suffocates joy and produces fear. Spirit-driven faith produces freedom and love. Paul's message is clear: do not trade the freedom Christ purchased for a burden he has already broken. Stand firm in the gospel. Freedom is your inheritance. Christ is your righteousness. And the Spirit is your hope.

APPLICATION

1. Christian freedom must be guarded, not assumed

Paul's command to "stand firm" shows that freedom is not automatic. Christians often think of freedom as a one-time gift rather than an ongoing posture. Yet Paul knows that even sincere Christians drift back into the comfort of rules, the approval of others, or the illusion of earning God's acceptance. When life feels uncertain, structure feels safer than trust. When

Christians slip into a performance mindset—measuring spiritual health by routines or comparing themselves to others—they begin carrying a burden Christ already lifted. Paul calls believers to active vigilance. Guarding freedom means examining motives, questioning where pressure comes from, and resisting the temptation to let anything compete with Christ as the foundation of righteousness. This vigilance is not fueled by fear but by gratitude: Christians fiercely protect the freedom Christ purchased because it is the very life he intends for them.

2. The temptation to trust religious performance is subtle but spiritually dangerous

Paul's warning about circumcision is not about one ritual—it is about the deeper impulse to trust personal effort. Today, this temptation can appear respectable: spiritual disciplines, moral consistency, heritage, ministry effort, or even doctrinal precision can become quiet replacements for reliance on Christ. None of these things are wrong, but when they become the basis for confidence before God, they turn into chains. Paul insists that trusting even a small part of the law for righteousness obligates a person to keep *all* of it. That path cannot produce life; it only exposes failure. Christians must ask themselves where they are tempted to supplement grace with effort. Freedom comes not from spiritual achievement but from surrender to Christ's finished work. When Christians rest in grace, obedience flows from joy rather than fear.

3. False teaching often spreads by appealing to fear and offering control

Paul's anger toward the false teachers is rooted in love for the Galatians. The agitators were not promoting obvious heresy—they were using persuasion, flattery, and religious seriousness to gain influence. Their message offered a sense of control: "Do this, and you'll be right with God." Fear and control always travel together. Christians today face similar pressures from voices that promise spiritual certainty through formulas, systems, or traditions. These messages are attractive because they reduce the Christian life to something manageable. But Paul warns that such teaching undermines the cross, removes the scandal of grace, and blinds Christians to their true freedom. Discernment is essential. Christians must learn to evaluate messages not by how persuasive, traditional, or disciplined they appear, but by whether they keep Christ at the center. Anything that shifts trust away from Jesus must be rejected, no matter how spiritual it seems.

4. Faith expresses itself not through obligation but through love empowered by the Spirit

Paul's phrase "faith working through love" captures the essence of Christian life. The law demands obedience out of obligation; the Spirit produces obedience out of love. When Christians live in the freedom Christ provides, they discover that love becomes the natural fruit of faith. This love is not sentimental. It is active, patient, sacrificial, and Spirit-driven. It grows not because Christians force themselves to be better but because the Spirit shapes their desires. Paul calls believers to stop asking, "What must I do to be accepted?" and start asking, "How can I love because I *am* accepted?" The first question leads back to slavery; the second springs from freedom. When Christians live in the grace that Christ provides, they find their hearts increasingly shaped by love—toward God, toward one another, and toward a world that needs the same freedom.

CONCLUSION

Galatians 5:1–12 is Paul at his clearest and most urgent. He wants the Galatians—and every Christian—to understand that the freedom Christ gives is not a small detail of the gospel; it is the heartbeat of the gospel. Christ did not set people free so they could drift back into the anxiety of earning righteousness through rule-keeping. He set them free so they could live in the confidence of his finished work, trusting that the Spirit will shape their lives from the inside out. Returning to the law may feel familiar, disciplined, or safe, but Paul insists it leads only back into slavery.

Paul's warnings are sharp because the danger is real. A single addition to the gospel can reshape everything. A single voice offering spiritual improvement apart from Christ can redirect an entire life. Yet beneath Paul's urgency is a steady hope: Christians who keep their eyes on Christ, who lean on the Spirit, and who resist every voice that competes with grace will stand firm in the freedom they have been given. Faith working through love—not law, not ritual, not performance—is the true expression of the Christian life.

REFLECTION

1. How does Paul's call to "stand firm" challenge the way you think about Christian freedom in your daily life?

2. Where do you feel the strongest pull toward relying on religious effort rather than grace?

3. How have small compromises or "little leaven" shaped your spiritual confidence in the past?

4. Which voices in your life most often hinder you from running well in the gospel?

5. How does remembering the Spirit's role in producing righteousness reshape your expectations of spiritual growth?

6. What does "faith working through love" reveal about the kind of life God desires for you?

DISCUSSION

1. Why does Paul describe returning to the law as submitting again to a "yoke of slavery"?

2. What makes circumcision such a powerful symbol in Paul's argument about law and grace?

3. How does Paul contrast the life of the Spirit with the life of the law in this passage?

4. What makes false teaching so persuasive, and why does Paul respond with such intensity?

5. How does the metaphor of running a race help explain the Galatians' spiritual drift?

6. Why does the cross offend those who want to rely on law, and what does this teach about the nature of grace?

11

KEEPING IN STEP WITH THE SPIRIT

GALATIANS 5:13-26

Objective: To show how Christian freedom is expressed through love, empowered by the Spirit, and evidenced by the fruit that reflects Christ's character.

INTRODUCTION

In 1947, a young man named Jackie Robinson stepped onto the field as the first Black player in modern Major League Baseball. The pressure was immense. Robinson faced open hostility, taunts from opposing players, icy silence from some teammates, and vicious treatment from fans. Brooklyn Dodgers executive Branch Rickey had warned him beforehand that breaking the color barrier would take more than athletic skill—it would require extraordinary restraint. Rickey asked Robinson a shocking question: "Can you have the guts not to fight back?"

Robinson agreed, not because he lacked strength, but because he understood the greater purpose. His restraint was not weakness; it was disciplined freedom. He had the right to respond in anger, but he chose a higher path so that something bigger could be accomplished. His self-control became a witness that changed the game and, in many ways, the nation.

Christians are truly free—freed from the burden of earning salvation and freed from the power of the law. But that freedom is not an invitation to indulge the flesh. It is the opportunity to display a different way of life, one shaped by the Spirit rather than by impulse. The Spirit forms in Christians a kind of freedom that looks like love, patience, gentleness, and self-control. Just as Robinson's disciplined restraint bore witness to a new era in baseball, Spirit-shaped character bears witness to the new life God creates in his people.

EXAMINATION

Galatians 5:13–26 is the practical heart of Paul's letter. After he has defended justification by faith, exposed the danger of returning to the law, and insisted on the importance of Christian freedom, Paul now turns to the natural question: What does freedom look like? The false teachers assumed that removing the law would lead to moral chaos. They feared that a life built on grace would produce lazy, careless Christians. Paul knows better. Freedom is not the absence of guidance—it is the presence of the Spirit. Freedom is not self-indulgence—it is the capacity to love. And freedom is not moral uncertainty—it is the Spirit producing the character of Christ in the hearts of God's people.

Paul begins with a remarkable statement: "You were called to freedom, brothers." He does not treat freedom as a reward earned through mature living or as a privilege granted to elite Christians. Freedom is the starting point of the Christian life. Christ did not set people free so they could slide back into fear or self-reliance. He set them free so they could finally live the life God intended—a life shaped not by external rules but by internal transformation.

Immediately after affirming their freedom, Paul offers a necessary warning: "Only do not use your freedom as an opportunity for the flesh." This clarifies a common misunderstanding. Spiritual freedom is not permission to indulge sinful desires. The "flesh" in Paul's writings refers not to the physical body but to the fallen human nature inclined toward self-centeredness. Freedom can be twisted if it turns inward. The danger is real: Christians can turn grace into an excuse to gratify desires that do not honor God. But Paul shows the antidote: "Through love serve one another." True freedom always bends outward. It expresses itself in self-giving love, not selfish indulgence.

Paul strengthens this point by summarizing the entire law in a single sentence: "You shall love your neighbor as yourself." Jesus himself taught this truth, and Paul echoes it here. Love does not abolish the law; it fulfills it. When Christians walk in love, they live in harmony with God's moral will without being under the legal system of the old covenant. The presence of the Spirit creates what the law could only describe.

But Paul knows the reality of the Galatians' situation. Their drift toward legalism had not produced unity; it had produced conflict. "If you bite and devour one another, watch out that you are not consumed by one another." Legalism fuels comparison, pride, and judgment. It destroys community. Paul warns that a church built on human effort eventually collapses under the weight of its own competitiveness. Freedom expressed through love, however, builds community.

Paul now moves to the center of Christian living: "Walk by the Spirit, and you will not gratify the desires of the flesh." This is not a technique—it is a relationship. The Spirit is not a vague force but the indwelling presence of God. To walk by the Spirit means to depend on him daily, trust his guidance, rely on his strength, and yield to his influence. The promise is remarkable: walking by the Spirit removes the power of the flesh. Christians do not defeat sin by sheer willpower but by following the Spirit.

Paul then describes the conflict that every Christian experiences. "For the desires of the flesh are against the Spirit, and the desires of the Spirit are against the flesh." This tension is not a sign of failure; it is evidence of spiritual life. Before conversion, there was no conflict—only the flesh ruling unchecked. After conversion, the Spirit enters the heart and creates a new desire for holiness. The conflict is real, ongoing, and intense, but it is also hopeful. Christians fight sin not alone, but with the Spirit who overcomes the flesh.

Paul adds an important clarification: "If you are led by the Spirit, you are not under the law." Walking by the Spirit does not lead Christians back into the law. The law cannot produce the life it commands. The Spirit produces the righteousness the law describes. Legalism cannot defeat the flesh; the Spirit can.

Paul now contrasts "the works of the flesh" with "the fruit of the Spirit." He begins with the works of the flesh—acts produced by sin when it rules a life. The list is broad and sobering: sexual immorality, impurity, sensuality, idolatry, sorcery, enmity, strife, jealousy, fits of anger, rivalries, dissensions, divisions, envy, drunkenness, and orgies. The list includes both scandalous sins and socially respectable ones. Paul includes sexual sins, spiritual sins, relational sins, and sins of excess. The common thread is self-centeredness. The flesh always turns inward and produces actions that tear down community, dishonor God, and enslave the individual.

Paul adds a serious warning: "Those who do such things will not inherit the kingdom of God." Paul is describing a lifestyle dominated by the flesh without repentance. Those who belong to Christ cannot remain at peace with the flesh.

Paul then turns to the fruit of the Spirit—a single fruit with nine qualities: love, joy, peace, patience, kindness, goodness, faithfulness, gentleness, and self-control. These qualities are not human achievements. They are evidence of the Spirit's work. They describe the character of Christ himself. Notice that Paul does not command Christians to produce fruit. He calls them to walk by the Spirit, and the fruit appears naturally. Obedience is essential, but it is grounded in reliance, not self-effort.

The traits of the Spirit stand in sharp contrast to the works of the flesh. Love replaces hostility. Joy replaces despair. Peace replaces anxiety and conflict. Patience replaces impulsiveness. Kindness replaces harshness. Goodness replaces self-serving choices. Faithfulness replaces unreliability. Gentleness replaces aggression. Self-control replaces indulgence. This fruit is not merely ethical—it is relational. It strengthens community and reflects God's character in daily life.

Paul then adds an intriguing phrase: "Against such things there is no law." No law is needed to restrain the fruit of the Spirit because these qualities fulfill God's moral will. The law's purpose was to restrain wrongdoing, but the Spirit's purpose is to produce righteousness.

Paul moves from character to identity: "Those who belong to Christ Jesus have crucified the flesh with its passions and desires." This is decisive language. At conversion, Christians decisively reject the flesh's authority. This does not mean the flesh is gone, but it has been dethroned. The Christian now lives by the Spirit. The battle continues, but the outcome is decided.

Paul concludes with a final exhortation: "If we live by the Spirit, let us also keep in step with the Spirit." Paul uses a military metaphor—march in rhythm with the Spirit's direction. Christians do not set the pace; they follow the Spirit's lead. He directs, guides, convicts, and empowers. Keeping in step means aligning one's priorities, habits, and desires with his work.

Paul ends with a relational warning: "Let us not become conceited, provoking one another, envying one another." Freedom without love leads to pride. Pride leads to comparison. Comparison leads to conflict. The Spirit leads away from these attitudes. The flesh produces rivalry; the Spirit produces unity.

Galatians 5:13–26 gives a comprehensive vision of Christian life. Freedom is the foundation. Love is the expression. The Spirit is the power. The flesh remains a threat, but the Spirit provides victory. The law cannot produce maturity, but the Spirit forms Christlike character. The gospel does not leave Christians in a moral vacuum; it places them in a living relationship with the Spirit, who shapes their desires, energizes their obedience, and produces the fruit that reveals Christ in them.

Freedom is not doing whatever one wants—it is the liberation to become who God created his children to be. And Paul insists that life in the Spirit is the only path that leads there.

APPLICATION

1. Freedom expresses itself through love, not self-indulgence

Paul's reminder that Christians are "called to freedom" corrects the common misunderstanding that freedom means doing whatever we want. The flesh always bends freedom inward—toward comfort, preference, and self-focus. But the Spirit bends freedom outward—toward service, compassion, and love. When Christians use grace as an excuse to indulge sinful desires, they distort the very freedom Christ purchased. But when Christians use their freedom to serve others, they display the gospel's power. This is why Paul grounds Christian ethics not in fear or rule-keeping but in love. Love fulfills the law because it reflects God's character. Practically, this means asking not, "What am I allowed to do?" but "How can my freedom bless someone else?" The more Christians lean into love, the more their freedom becomes a testimony to Christ rather than a cover for the flesh.

2. The battle between flesh and Spirit requires daily dependence on God

Paul's description of the conflict between flesh and Spirit explains a reality every Christian feels. The flesh pulls toward self-centeredness, anger, escapism, impurity, and pride. The Spirit pulls toward holiness, patience, gentleness, and faith. This tension is not evidence of spiritual failure; it is evidence of spiritual life. Before Christ, the flesh ruled without resistance. After Christ, the Spirit enters the heart and awakens new desires that oppose the old ones. But victory does not come through gritting one's teeth. It comes through walking by the Spirit—depending on him in prayer, listening to his Word, confessing sin honestly, and yielding to his prompting. Spiritual maturity is not the absence of struggle; it is learning to rely on the Spirit rather than on our own strength. Each day becomes an invitation to choose the Spirit's lead instead of the flesh's impulses.

3. The fruit of the Spirit reveals Christ's character growing in us

Paul's contrast between the works of the flesh and the fruit of the Spirit shows the difference between behaviors we produce and character God produces. Works of the flesh arise naturally when the heart is disconnected from God—they are the default setting of fallen humanity. They divide churches, damage relationships, and enslave those who practice them. By contrast, the fruit of the Spirit is not a list of tasks to complete but the evidence of Christ's life taking shape within us. Love, joy, peace, patience, kindness, goodness, faithfulness, gentleness, and self-control are not self-improvement goals; they are supernatural marks of transformation. Christians pursue spiritual disciplines not to manufacture fruit but to stay connected to the One who produces it. As the Spirit changes our desires, we slowly begin to respond to people, pressure, and suffering the way Christ does. This fruit is the visible signature of a Spirit-led life.

4. Keeping in step with the Spirit shapes community, not just personal behavior

Paul ends the section by warning against conceit, provocation, and envy—sins that fracture relationships. This shows that life in the Spirit is not merely about private holiness; it is about shared fellowship. The flesh always pushes believers toward comparison and competition. The Spirit leads them toward humility, patience, and unity. To "keep in step with the Spirit" means aligning our actions and attitudes with the Spirit's rhythm, especially in how we treat one another. It means refusing to demand our own way, resisting the urge to judge, and choosing gentleness when conflict arises. Spirit-led community is marked by mutual encouragement, forgiveness, and a shared desire to reflect Christ together. When a church walks in step with the Spirit, its relationships become living illustrations of the gospel—marked not by rivalry or pride but by the love and unity that only the Spirit can produce.

CONCLUSION

Galatians 5:13–26 reveals that Christian freedom is more than release from the law—it is the invitation to a life shaped by the Spirit. Paul makes clear that grace does not lead to self-indulgence. It leads to love. The Spirit does not leave Christians to wrestle with the flesh alone. He creates new desires, gives strength in the daily conflict, and produces fruit that no rule or ritual could ever generate. The works of the flesh divide and destroy, but the fruit of the Spirit builds, heals, and reflects the character of Christ.

Paul calls Christians to take freedom seriously—not as a license to do whatever they want, but as a calling to live as God's image-bearers in a broken world. Walking by the Spirit means learning to trust his leading, depend on his power, and let him shape both personal character and community life. In the end, freedom finds its fullest expression in love empowered by the Spirit, not in the desires of the flesh.

REFLECTION

1. How does Paul's command to "serve one another through love" reshape your understanding of what Christian freedom is for?

2. Where do you personally sense the strongest pull of the flesh, and how might walking by the Spirit redirect those desires?

3. Which fruit of the Spirit has God been growing in you recently, and which one do you most need to pray for?

4. How does the ongoing conflict between flesh and Spirit encourage you rather than discourage you?

5. What relationships in your life would look different if you kept more closely "in step with the Spirit"?

6. How does remembering that the Spirit—not the law—produces true holiness change your approach to spiritual growth?

DISCUSSION

1. Why does Paul warn the Galatians not to use their freedom as an opportunity for the flesh?

2. How does loving one another fulfill the law in ways the law itself could never accomplish?

3. What does Paul mean by "walk by the Spirit," and how is that different from following rules?

4. Why does Paul list both scandalous sins and socially acceptable ones under "works of the flesh"?

5. How does the metaphor of "fruit" help us understand the Spirit's role in producing Christlike character?

6. Why does Paul end with warnings against provocation and envy? What does this teach about the communal nature of life in the Spirit?

12

A COMMUNITY SHAPED BY THE SPIRIT

GALATIANS 6:1-10

Objective: To show how the Spirit forms a community marked by
gentleness, shared burdens, personal responsibility,
and perseverance in doing good.

INTRODUCTION

In 1945, during the final months of World War II, American soldiers liberated the concentration camp at Dachau. What they found was overwhelming—thousands of prisoners starving, sick, and too weak to stand. Medical personnel were rushed in, and one of them, Captain Marcus J. Smith, later wrote about the overwhelming challenge. The prisoners needed food, clothing, medicine, and emotional stability. But the number of doctors and nurses was small, and the suffering was immense.

Smith noticed something remarkable: the prisoners began helping one another. Former inmates who had regained a measure of strength carried those who could not walk. Others spoon-fed those too weak to lift their hands. Some comforted the dying while others cleaned wounds or translated instructions. Smith later said their survival during those first days was possible only because "they lifted each other's burdens with a devotion I had rarely seen." He observed that physical care alone wasn't enough—the survivors needed a community working together if healing was going to happen.

Paul describes a similar kind of spiritual care in Galatians 6:1–10. Christians are called to restore the fallen, carry one another's loads, watch over their own hearts, sow to the Spirit, and persevere in doing good. No believer heals alone, grows alone, or endures alone. A Spirit-shaped community becomes a place where burdens are lifted, wounds are tended, and restoration is pursued with gentleness and humility.

EXAMINATION

As Paul nears the end of his letter, he turns from theological correction to practical guidance. Galatians 6:1–10 shows what a community shaped by the Spirit actually looks like. Paul has spent an entire letter arguing that Christians are not under the law, that righteousness comes through faith, that the Spirit produces the fruit of Christlike character, and that believers must keep in step with the Spirit. Now he shows what Spirit-led life looks like *together*, in relationships marked by gentleness, humility, responsibility, generosity, and perseverance.

Paul begins with the scenario no church can avoid: "If anyone is caught in any transgression…" The question is not *whether* Christians sin but how Christians respond *when* sin appears. The legalists in Galatia would handle it harshly, with judgment and distance. Paul takes the opposite approach. "You who are spiritual should restore him in a spirit of gentleness." "Spiritual" here refers not to elite Christians but to any believer walking by the Spirit as described in the previous chapter.

Restoration is not passive; it is active care. The word "restore" carries the idea of mending a torn net or setting a broken bone—actions done carefully, patiently, and with the goal of healing. The goal is not exposure, punishment, or shame. The goal is wholeness. Even the gentleness Paul calls for reflects the fruit of the Spirit. Christians who have received grace restore others with grace.

But Paul immediately adds a warning: "Keep watch on yourself, lest you too be tempted." Restoration requires humility and self-awareness. The restorer is not superior to the one who fell. Christians are vulnerable to the same failures, and the awareness of shared weakness keeps restoration from becoming condescension. Paul knows that spiritual pride is a danger even in good works. Helping someone else can subtly shift into self-congratulation unless believers guard their hearts.

From restoration, Paul moves to the broader picture of burden-bearing: "Bear one another's burdens, and so fulfill the law of Christ." Though Christians are free from the law of Moses, they remain under the law of Christ—the law of love. Burdens come in endless forms: grief, financial strain, temptation, anxiety, illness, discouragement, relational conflict, spiritual confusion. The Spirit does not call Christians to live isolated or self-sufficient lives. He creates a community where people carry loads together. Burden-bearing is not occasional charity; it is a way of life shaped by Christ's example of self-giving love.

Yet immediately after urging mutual care, Paul adds, "If anyone thinks he is something, when he is nothing, he deceives himself." Pride destroys community. Comparison destroys fellowship. Thinking of oneself as too important to assist the struggling or too mature to receive correction undermines the very heart of the gospel. Paul calls Christians to a sober understanding of themselves—not groveling self-hatred, but realistic humility. The Spirit reminds believers that they are recipients, not achievers, of grace.

Paul then writes, "Let each one test his own work." This does not contradict burden-bearing; it complements it. Christians are responsible for their choices, motives, and actions. "Testing" means evaluating the quality of one's obedience, not in comparison to others but in light of Christ. Paul says this leads to rejoicing "in himself alone and not in his neighbor." This rejoicing is not pride but satisfaction in faithful obedience prompted by the Spirit.

Then Paul adds, "For each will have to bear his own load." Paul uses a different word here than the burden of verse 2. The "load" refers to personal responsibility—what God assigns each person. Christians cannot carry someone else's discipleship for them. They cannot excise someone else's temptations, take someone else's tests, or live someone else's life. Mutual support and personal accountability live side by side. Christians help one another, but each must answer to God for their own obedience.

Paul then shifts to the topic of generosity, though still within the theme of responsibility: "Let the one who is taught the word share all good things with the one who teaches." This reflects the early Christian understanding that spiritual instruction has value and that those who teach depend on the support of the community. Paul is not demanding wealth for teachers; he is emphasizing partnership in ministry. Sharing "all good things" means material support, encouragement, hospitality, and appreciation. A Spirit-led church honors those who labor in the Word.

Next, Paul introduces one of the most memorable principles in the letter: "Do not be deceived: God is not mocked, for whatever one sows, that will he also reap." This principle applies broadly, but Paul applies it specifically to spiritual investment. Sowing involves daily choices—habits, priorities, desires, and actions. Reaping reflects the long-term consequences of those choices. Grace never erases responsibility. A Christian cannot sow selfishness, anger, impurity, or neglect of the Spirit and expect spiritual health. The pattern of sowing and reaping stands as a warning and as an encouragement.

Paul draws the contrast sharply: "The one who sows to his own flesh will from the flesh reap corruption." The flesh produces decay: fractured relationships, drained joy, shallow faith, and spiritual stagnation. But "the one who sows to the Spirit will from the Spirit reap eternal life." Eternal life here is not merely future life but the life of the age to come—the quality of life shaped by the Spirit, full of love, peace, joy, and communion with God. Sowing to the Spirit means investing in what aligns with God's character—prayer, Scripture, worship, generosity, service, repentance, accountability, obedience, and love.

Paul then acknowledges what every Christian knows: sowing to the Spirit requires perseverance. "And let us not grow weary of doing good, for in due season we will reap, if we do not give up." Doing good—restoring the fallen, bearing burdens, resisting the flesh, encouraging teachers, practicing generosity—can be exhausting. Paul does not shame the weary; he encourages them. The harvest is certain. The Spirit is faithful. The reward is real. Christians sow in hope because God gives the growth.

Paul concludes with a broad exhortation: "So then, as we have opportunity, let us do good to everyone, and especially to those who are of the household of faith." Spirit-shaped love extends outward to all people, but Paul shows that the family of God has a special claim on Christians' attention. We cannot meet every need in the world, but we can faithfully do good wherever God gives opportunity—beginning with the brothers and sisters God has placed closest to us.

Galatians 6:1–10 offers a vision of a community where the Spirit shapes every relationship. In contrast to the competitive, divisive spirit produced by the flesh, the Spirit produces gentleness, humility, generosity, responsibility, and perseverance. Restoration replaces condemnation. Burden-bearing replaces pride. Personal responsibility replaces comparison. Generosity replaces neglect. Perseverance replaces weariness.

This passage reminds Christians that life in the Spirit is not merely personal; it is profoundly communal. The Spirit forms a people—not just individuals—who reflect the love and character of Christ in tangible ways. Paul's call is clear: Spirit-led people restore gently, carry faithfully, judge humbly, sow wisely, and persevere boldly. This is the life to which the gospel calls the church—a life that reflects Jesus in every relationship.

APPLICATION

1. Restoration must be gentle, intentional, and grounded in humility

Paul's instruction to "restore" a fallen brother or sister highlights one of the most delicate tasks within a church. Restoration is neither ignoring sin nor crushing the sinner—it is the careful work of helping someone return to spiritual health. This requires the gentleness produced by the Spirit, not the harshness produced by pride. Christians often underestimate how vulnerable someone is after being caught in sin. Shame, fear, and confusion can make a person feel isolated or hopeless. That is why Paul says to "keep watch" over ourselves while restoring others. The moment we think we are above the same temptation, we lose the posture required for genuine help. Gentle restoration means entering another's struggle with patience, prayer, and compassion, knowing that we too depend on grace every day. When a church embraces this spirit, it becomes a place of healing rather than fear—a community where brokenness is met with hope.

2. Spirit-led community carries burdens together while honoring personal responsibility

Paul holds two truths together: Christians must help bear one another's burdens, and Christians must carry their own load. The first truth guards against isolation. Every Christian will face seasons of heaviness—grief, temptation, anxiety, financial strain, or relational hurt. Spirit-led believers do not merely offer sympathy; they come alongside, lift weight, and walk with those who are struggling. The second truth guards against passivity. Each Christian still has responsibilities God has assigned—spiritual growth, repentance, obedience, stewardship—that no one else can fulfill for them. Healthy community avoids two extremes: expecting others to carry everything for us or refusing to let anyone near our struggles. Spirit-led churches hold these truths in tension, creating relationships of shared strength and personal accountability. When Christians carry burdens together and also own their calling before God, they reflect Christ, who both carried our greatest burden and calls us to follow him faithfully.

3. What we sow spiritually today shapes who we become tomorrow

Paul's principle of sowing and reaping is both a warning and an encouragement. Every choice—large or small—plants a seed. Sowing to the flesh means cultivating habits that feed pride, anger, impurity, laziness, or selfishness. Over time, these seeds grow into patterns that damage relationships and sap spiritual vitality. Sowing to the Spirit means investing in practices that open our hearts to God's transforming work—prayer, Scripture, worship, service, confession, generosity, and dependence. These seeds grow slowly but steadily into the fruit of Christlike character. Paul urges Christians not to deceive themselves: spiritual growth is not accidental. It is the cumulative result of countless daily decisions. The promise is that God honors Spirit-led sowing. Though the harvest may seem distant, he assures Christians that perseverance will bear fruit. When believers invest intentionally in the Spirit's work, they cultivate a life marked by stability, strength, and joy.

4. Perseverance in doing good is essential to Spirit-shaped community

Paul acknowledges what every Christian understands: doing good can become exhausting. Carrying burdens, restoring the fallen, giving generously, resisting the flesh, and investing in others all require emotional and spiritual energy. Weariness sets in when results seem slow or when gratitude is absent. That is why Paul says, "Let us not grow weary… for in due season we will reap." He does not deny the fatigue—he speaks into it. Perseverance is not powered by sheer determination but by remembering the certainty of God's harvest. Christians sow in faith, trusting that God uses every act of kindness, every moment of patience, every sacrifice of time or resources. And the scope of doing good is wide: "to everyone," with special attention to "the household of faith." Spirit-shaped perseverance creates a community where grace is not occasional but consistent—where love is practiced not just when convenient but as a way of life that echoes Christ's endurance on our behalf.

CONCLUSION

Galatians 6:1–10 paints a picture of what the gospel produces when it takes root in a community. The Spirit does not simply transform individual hearts—he forms a people who care for one another with the humility and gentleness of Christ. Instead of harsh judgment, there is restoration. Instead of isolation, there is burden-bearing. Instead of pride, there is sober self-awareness. Instead of spiritual neglect, there is intentional sowing to the Spirit. And instead of weariness leading to resignation, there is hopeful perseverance grounded in God's promise of a harvest.

Paul wants Christians to see that life in the Spirit is not abstract or theoretical. It is lived out in kitchens, hospital rooms, living rooms, fellowship halls, and daily relationships. When Christians walk by the Spirit together, the church becomes a place of healing, strength, and endurance—a community that reflects the character of Christ and displays his love to the world.

REFLECTION

1. How does Paul's call to restore the fallen with gentleness challenge the way you think about helping others who struggle with sin?

2. What burdens in your life do you need to invite others to help carry—and whose burdens might God be calling you to share?

3. Where do you see pride or comparison creeping into your relationships, making it harder to test your own work humbly?

4. How does the principle of sowing and reaping help you evaluate the habits, priorities, and choices shaping your spiritual life right now?

5. What keeps you from sowing more intentionally to the Spirit, and how might you lean on God's grace to change that pattern?

6. Where do you feel weary in doing good, and how does Paul's promise of a future harvest encourage you to persevere?

DISCUSSION

1. What does Paul's instruction to "restore" someone in a "spirit of gentleness" teach us about the tone and posture of Christian correction?

2. How do verses 2 and 5 work together—carrying each other's burdens while also bearing our own loads?

3. What dangers arise when a church fails to practice humility and instead entertains comparison or conceit?

4. How does the principle of sowing and reaping help Christians understand both the seriousness of sin and the hope of spiritual growth?

5. In what ways does the call to "do good to everyone, especially to the household of faith" challenge the priorities of the modern church?

6. How does this passage show that life in the Spirit is deeply communal rather than individualistic?

13

BOASTING ONLY IN THE CROSS

GALATIANS 6:11–18

Objective: To call Christians to reject shallow markers of spirituality, boast only in the cross, and live as God's new creation through grace.

INTRODUCTION

In 1857, a brilliant young mathematician named Évariste Galois stood before a Parisian exam board. Galois possessed one of the most creative mathematical minds of his era; the theories he developed would later revolutionize modern algebra. But the examiners misunderstood him entirely. They judged him harshly—not because his work lacked depth, but because it did not fit their expectations. His methods were unconventional, his explanations unpolished, and his thinking too bold for the academic structures of his day.

Galois died tragically young, but his notes—scribbled in frantic handwriting the night before his death—became some of the most celebrated mathematical insights in history. What the examiners dismissed, the world eventually recognized as genius. Their criteria were too small to measure the value of his work. Only later did others realize that Galois had been operating on an entirely different level.

Paul speaks similarly in Galatians 6:11–18. The false teachers judged spirituality by outward markers—circumcision, ritual, appearance, and reputation. They measured faith with criteria too small for the gospel. But Paul insists that the true sign of God's people is not in the flesh but in the cross and in the new creation God brings about through Christ. What the world calls weakness is God's power. What the world calls foolish is God's wisdom. And what the world overlooks—grace, suffering, humble faithfulness—is the very evidence of authentic Christian identity.

EXAMINATION

As Paul brings his letter to a close, he picks up the pen himself. "See with what large letters I am writing to you with my own hand." In the ancient world, dictation was common—scribes wrote as the author spoke. But at key moments, an author might add his own handwriting to underline urgency, authenticity, or affection. Paul's large letters are not due to poor eyesight alone; they signal the gravity of his final words. Galatians is not a casual letter. It is a spiritual rescue mission, and Paul wants his handwriting to carry the full weight of his passion.

Paul begins his final appeal by exposing the motives of the false teachers one last time. "It is those who want to make a good showing in the flesh who would force you to be circumcised." The phrase "make a good showing" refers to outward religious performance. Their interest was not the Galatians' spiritual health but their own reputation. In the Roman world, circumcision was controversial; for Jews, it remained a badge of honor. By persuading Gentile Christians to adopt it, these teachers could boast to their peers back home that they had expanded the Jewish identity of the churches. Their teaching was not driven by theological conviction but by fear—fear of persecution and fear of losing social standing. They wanted Christianity to look safer, more respectable, and more acceptable to their peers.

Paul adds another layer: "They desire to have you circumcised so that they may boast in your flesh." Their spiritual authority depended on visible proof. Circumcision gave them something to count, display, and parade as evidence of ministry success. Paul sees this as deeply destructive. Anytime religious leaders use people as statistics, badges, or trophies, they betray the heart of the gospel. True ministry does not collect bodies for display; it nurtures souls for Christ.

In contrast to their superficial motives, Paul offers his own: "But far be it from me to boast except in the cross of our Lord Jesus Christ." This is one of the most striking sentences Paul ever wrote. The Roman world viewed the cross with horror. It was an instrument of shame, humiliation, and public degradation. No one boasted in crosses. Yet Paul says the cross is his only boast. He wants nothing else to define him—not heritage, not achievements, not suffering, not influence, not status, not religious accomplishments. The cross is the entire reason for his identity, hope, and mission.

Why the cross? Because the cross is where God decisively revealed the truth about salvation, humanity, and grace. At the cross, Christ bore the curse of the law. There, he fulfilled the promise to Abraham. There, he broke the power of sin. There, he set humanity free from the crushing burden of self-salvation. The cross shatters the illusion that righteousness can be earned. It exposes the futility of legalism. It demolishes religious pride. And it replaces all grounds for boasting with a single truth: Christians belong to God only because Christ gave himself for them.

Paul continues: "By which the world has been crucified to me, and I to the world." The "world" in Paul's writings refers to the human system of values built on power, achievement, status, and pride—everything that people use to measure worth apart from God. Through the cross, Paul declares that this world no longer controls him. Its approval does not entice him; its disapproval does not intimidate him. The world's categories do not define him. Its standards do not guide him. Its rewards do not impress him. And because Paul is crucified to the world, the world finds no place in him. His allegiance is to Christ alone.

Paul then makes one of the most important theological statements in Galatians: "For neither circumcision counts for anything, nor uncircumcision, but a new creation." After six chapters of argument, correction, and pleading, Paul reaches the heart of the matter. The true marker of God's people is not ritual, heritage, or identity markers—Jewish or Gentile, traditional or nontraditional, conservative or progressive. What matters is the new creation.

The new creation is the transforming work of God in the heart through the Spirit. It is the fulfillment of Old Testament promises—God giving a new heart, a new spirit, a restored humanity. It is the beginning of the new world God is creating through Christ. Circumcision and uncircumcision are irrelevant because they belong to the old order of things. In the new creation, what counts is whether someone has been united with Christ, indwelt by the Spirit, and changed from the inside out.

Paul then speaks a blessing: "As for all who walk by this rule, peace and mercy be upon them, and upon the Israel of God." The "rule" is the guideline he just stated: the cross and the new creation. Those who embrace this truth—Jew or Gentile—receive peace and mercy. Paul calls them "the Israel of God," a phrase with deep theological significance. He is not redefining Israel politically or ethnically; he is describing the people who truly belong to God through faith in Christ. They are the heirs of Abraham's promise, the fulfillment of God's covenant, and the community shaped by the Spirit rather than by the law.

Paul's final personal note is equally powerful: "From now on let no one cause me trouble, for I bear on my body the marks of Jesus." While the false teachers wanted to boast in the flesh of the Galatians, Paul bears actual scars—bruises from beatings, marks from stonings, wounds from persecution. These scars are not badges of honor, but they are real evidence of loyalty. They reveal that Paul's ministry is not built on ease, applause, or prestige. The marks he carries show that the cross is not just a message he preaches—it is a reality he lives. He belongs to Christ, and his scars prove his sincerity far more than any ritual ever could.

Paul's final sentence is a fitting conclusion: "The grace of our Lord Jesus Christ be with your spirit, brothers." He ends where he began—with grace. After all the rebukes, warnings, appeals, and corrections, Paul ends with blessing, affection, and a call to unity. Grace is what launched the Christian life, what sustains it, what shapes community, and what empowers the Spirit's work. Grace is the final word because grace is the only foundation of the gospel.

Galatians 6:11–18 shows Paul's heart laid bare. He contrasts the shallow motives of those who seek reputation with the deep sacrifice of those who follow Christ. He contrasts outward markers of holiness with the inward reality of new creation. He contrasts human boasting with the singular boast of the cross. And he contrasts superficial religion with the grace that forms true disciples.

This closing paragraph gathers the entire letter into one final call: Let the cross be your only boast. Let the new creation be your identity. Let grace be your atmosphere.

APPLICATION

1. The cross—not achievement—is the center of Christian identity

Paul's declaration that he will boast in nothing but the cross confronts every Christian with a searching question: *What truly defines me?* The flesh loves to build identity on accomplishments—career success, moral track record, religious activity, or the approval of others. But the cross dismantles every form of self-reliance. It reveals that righteousness cannot be earned and that salvation comes only through Christ's sacrifice. When Christians root their identity in the cross, they become people marked by humility rather than pride, confidence rather than insecurity, and gratitude rather than self-congratulation. This perspective also reshapes how Christians respond to failure: the cross assures them they are not defined by their worst moments. And it reshapes how they respond to success: the cross reminds them that grace is their foundation. Learning to boast in the cross means refusing to let anything else—not achievement, not reputation, not religious performance—determine worth.

2. False motives must be recognized and resisted

Paul exposes the false teachers' motives because motives always matter. They wanted circumcision not to honor God but to enhance their reputation and avoid persecution. Their "success" depended on using people as proof of their influence. This dynamic still appears today, not only in overtly manipulative leaders but in more subtle ways—when ministries care more about numbers than souls, when Christians pursue approval rather than authenticity, when leaders measure success by visibility rather than faithfulness. Paul's words teach Christians to evaluate not just messages but motives. Spiritual influence that flows from pride, fear, or self-protection always harms others. True ministry aims for transformation, not trophies. It lifts up Christ instead of elevating personalities. Christians must cultivate discernment—asking whether a teacher's message leads them to dependence on Christ or dependence on human structures. The gospel calls believers to reject every voice that—like the agitators in Galatia—appeals to the flesh instead of pointing to the cross.

3. The new creation is the true measure of spiritual life

Paul reminds the Galatians that neither circumcision nor uncircumcision matters—only a new creation. This confronts the tendency to evaluate spirituality by outward markers: strictness, looseness, tradition, innovation, emotion, intellect, or personal background. The gospel shifts the focus from externals to transformation. The new creation is God's work, not ours—the Spirit reshaping desires, renewing the mind, softening pride, healing wounds, and cultivating Christlike character. This perspective humbles Christians who are tempted to measure themselves by comparison, and it comforts those who feel inadequate because they lack certain religious experiences or traditions. The question is not "What external marks do I have?" but "Is Christ being formed in me?" The new creation becomes both a safeguard against legalism and a call to genuine holiness. Christians learn to value what God values: inward renewal, not outward performance; the Spirit's fruit, not human badges; transformation, not appearance.

4. Authentic discipleship embraces sacrifice rather than seeking applause

Paul contrasts the false teachers' desire for praise with his own scars—the "marks of Jesus" on his body. While they boasted in the flesh of others, Paul carried wounds from his own faithfulness. Authentic Christian living still requires this kind of courage. Following Christ means embracing paths that may not bring admiration: speaking truth when it is unpopular, serving quietly without recognition, forgiving when it feels costly, and choosing integrity over comfort. Many Christians today face pressure to shape their faith around cultural approval or personal ease, but Paul invites Christians to a deeper kind of discipleship—one that holds loosely to reputation and tightly to Christ. His scars remind believers that spiritual credibility is not earned through outward symbols but through faithful endurance. When Christians willingly bear the cost of obedience, they reflect the crucified Savior they follow. The church is strengthened not by flashy commitments, but by those who quietly carry the marks of belonging to Jesus.

CONCLUSION

Galatians 6:11–18 brings the entire letter to its rightful climax: everything Paul has argued—from justification by faith to the gift of the Spirit, from freedom in Christ to the danger of returning to the law—leads to the singular truth that the cross and the new creation are the only markers that matter. The false teachers boasted in outward symbols, but Paul boasts in the crucified Messiah who ended the old order and brought the new. The world that once shaped identity has been crucified with Christ, and a new world has begun in him.

Paul's final words remind Christians that true spirituality cannot be measured by ritual, performance, or reputation. It is seen in a life shaped by grace, in a heart renewed by the Spirit, and in a willingness to follow Jesus even when it requires sacrifice. The cross defines who Christians are; the new creation defines who they are becoming. And grace—always grace—remains the atmosphere in which they live.

REFLECTION

1. How does boasting only in the cross challenge the ways you normally define yourself or measure spiritual maturity?

2. Where do you notice the temptation to seek approval, reputation, or spiritual "success" the way the false teachers did?

3. What does it look like, in your life, to view the world as "crucified" to you—and you to the world?

4. How does the idea of the "new creation" encourage you when you feel spiritually inadequate or discouraged?

5. Which of Paul's "marks of Jesus" resonates most with you as a picture of authentic Christian faithfulness?

6. How does Paul's closing emphasis on grace shape the way you want to live and serve in the week ahead?

DISCUSSION

1. Why does Paul consider circumcision and uncircumcision equally irrelevant when it comes to belonging to God?

2. How do the false teachers' motives reveal deeper dangers than their teaching alone?

3. What does it mean for Christians to boast only in the cross, and why is this theme fitting for Paul's closing words?

4. How does Paul's emphasis on the new creation complete the argument of the entire letter?

5. Why does Paul point to his scars as evidence of his sincerity? What contrast is he making with the false teachers?

6. How does this passage reaffirm the central message of Galatians about grace, freedom, and the Spirit's work?

www.ingramcontent.com/pod-product-compliance
Lightning Source LLC
Chambersburg PA
CBHW070128030426
42335CB00016B/2301